EXTR~~E~~
LEFT A~~~~

West, Elmer (ed.) EXTREMISM
LEFT AND RIGHT, Eerdmans,
Grand Rapids, 1972.

EXTREMISM
LEFT AND RIGHT

edited by

ELMER S. WEST, JR.

WILLIAM B. EERDMANS PUBLISHING COMPANY

Grand Rapids, Michigan

Copyright © 1972 by William B. Eerdmans Publishing Company
All rights reserved
Library of Congress Catalog Card No.: 73-142902
ISBN 0-8028-1369-0
Printed in the United States of America

Contents

	Preface	7
1.	*The Anatomy of Extremism: Right and Left* by Henlee H. Barnette	9
2.	*Common Features of Extremism's Ugly Faces* by H. Clayton Waddell	28
3.	*Who's Who Among the Extremists* by G. Willis Bennett	44
4.	*Sources of Extremism* by C. Arthur Insko	59
5.	*Psychological Dimensions of Extremism* by C. W. Scudder	76
6.	*Tactics of Extremists* by John C. Howell	90
7.	*Extremists and the Mass Media* by Thomas A. Bland	105
8.	*The Gospel and Extremism* by Thomas A. Bland	120
9.	*Christians Coping with Extremism* by William M. Pinson, Jr.	132

Preface

These pages represent the best research and thinking of eight distinguished seminary professors of Christian ethics as they deal forthrightly with the explosive issue of extremism.

The primary purpose of the book is to expose extremism. The writers share the conviction that, regardless of the form its expressions may take, whether left or right, extremism represents a seedbed from which both vicious attitudes and violent actions spring. It is a multi-headed monster, too long unchallenged by the church.

The writers are not dealing with extremism in terms of its more positive aspects which have characterized committed leaders of religious, social, and political movements throughout history. Rather, they are calling upon us to face up to an insidious threat to the very fabric of our society which, for lack of a more adequate definition, has been labeled *extremism* by the mass media.

As in the case of some other words which have historically carried both positive and negative meanings, extremism in our day has been robbed of its more noble implications. Henlee Barnette points out in the opening chapter that many would call Jesus an extremist but contends that he was not, in the sense in which the word is now used, since "His extremism was related to love, not hate; faith, not fear; the dignity of man, not his dehumanization."

These chapters were first delivered as spoken messages at summer conferences in Glorieta, New Mexico, and Ridgecrest, North Carolina, sponsored by The Christian Life Commission of the Southern Baptist Convention. Shunning favoritism for one type of extremism over another, these probing inquiries give serious consideration to expressions of dedication gone overboard both to the left and to the right. In addition to critical analysis, there is a positive word of hope that as Christians commit themselves to the revolution called for by the gospel, they will help eliminate most of the sociological factors that create extremism.

Special appreciation is expressed to Foy Valentine, Executive Secretary of The Christian Life Commission, whose wise counsel was invaluable from beginning to end, and to Mrs. Pauline Barnard and Mrs. Faye Russell, whose careful scrutiny, helpful changes, and accurate typing brought the final manuscript to completion.

This book provides information about some of the dangers we face from extremism and how to cope with them. It is hoped that it will stimulate Christians to work more diligently for the reformation and renewal of basic institutions in society that they may better serve the purposes of God and the needs of men.

—Elmer S. West, Jr.

1

The Anatomy of Extremism: Right and Left

Henlee H. Barnette

Anatomy as a discipline has to do with dissecting a plant or an animal to determine the positions of its parts and their relation to one another. To study the anatomy of the body politic, we must analyze its structures, their functions, and their relation to each other. At each end of the social spectrum are extremist groups, and there is a large segment in the middle that is relatively soporific and stable. This study is focused primarily upon the extremist parts of the body politic.

The Semantics of "Extremism"

For a number of reasons the term "extremism" is a troublesome one for the semanticist. It is a slippery word, meaning different things to different people, and it is charged with highly emotional content. Moreover, though it is an old word, "extremism" has taken on a new meaning for most of us, expressive of the mood of our time but so far not given in a dictionary. Hence, it is difficult to find the precise meaning of the term.

Roget's Thesaurus lists more than one hundred cognates of the word "extremeness." Dictionary definitions

---

Henlee H. Barnette is Professor of Christian Ethics, Southern Baptist Theological Seminary, Louisville, Kentucky.

state that extremism is the quality or state of going to extremes. "Extreme" comes from the Latin *extremus*, meaning the outermost or last. An extremist, then, is excessive, immoderate, in his views and actions. The extremist advances to the outermost limits in ideology and practice.

"Fanatic" and "radical" are synonyms of "extremist." A fanatic, observed Winston Churchill, is "one who can't change his mind and won't change the subject." George Santayana declared, "Fanaticism consists in redoubling your efforts when you have forgotten your aim."[1] As for the radical, Franklin D. Roosevelt defined him in a radio speech on October 26, 1939, as "a man with both feet firmly planted in the air." During the 1964 presidential campaign, one popular label for an extremist was "a guy who keeps his socks up by walking on his hands."

Both Democratic and Republican leaders accused each other of harboring extremists in their respective parties during the Johnson-Goldwater campaign. In his acceptance speech at the Republican National Convention, Goldwater had declared: "I would remind you that extremism in defense of liberty is no vice. And let me remind you, also, that moderation in pursuit of justice is no virtue."

As a result of this ambiguous syllogism, Goldwater was attacked by defeated Republican leaders who charged that he was upholding everything from the John Birch Society to the Ku Klux Klan. Yet Dr. Martin Luther King, Jr., could quote Goldwater, for he, along with other clergymen, believed that "extremism in the defense of liberty is no vice," even to the point of disobeying what they believed were morally unjust laws. Moreover, the gradualism reflected in the courts and legislative bodies of the nation was held by King to be an indefensible kind of "moderation in the pursuit of justice."

It is necessary to bear in mind that the labels "left" and "right" refer to positions on a continuous spectrum.

---

[1] George Santayana, *Reason in Common Sense*, vol. I (New York: Collier Books, 1962), p. 22.

Toward the ends of the scale are points which are designated as extremist positions. In between are to be found less extreme postures. And whether or not a position on the spectrum is considered extreme depends upon who is making the judgment. Hence it is difficult to arrive at any precise notion of who is an extremist. But, generally speaking, the center of the spectrum represents the consensus of most Americans. On each side of the center are varying degrees of leftist and rightist stances.

Obviously, any attempt to define extremism with finality is hazardous. If one is granted the right to define his own terms, he can define anything. One can make a cherry pie out of red marbles if he defines red marbles as cherries. But to avoid becoming lost in a semantical swamp, it is necessary to articulate an operational definition of extremism which at least approximates its meaning.

The definitions given by two scholars are helpful. Wayne E. Oates declares: "*Extremism is an individual or group reaction against threat.* The sense of threat is out of keeping with reality. Extremism is an over-response to the structures of the threatening agent. Therefore, extremism represents symbolically the distorted and infected personal needs of the extremists."[2] J. M. Snapper refers to extremism as "a style of life" growing out of "certain patterns of child rearing and coming to expression particularly in times of personal and social strain and in ways varying with circumstances of issue, place, and time."[3] Basically it is a flight from fear of self and of other selves.[4]

Taken together, these definitions include both the psychological and social dimensions of extremism. Both are essential to an adequate understanding of the extremist. Therefore, we shall define extremism as *a style*

---

[2] Wayne E. Oates, *Pastoral Counseling in Social Problems* (Philadelphia: Westminster Press, 1966), p. 37.

[3] J. M. Snapper, "Extremism, A Style of Life," *The Reformed Journal*, January, 1965, p. 19.

[4] *Ibid.*

of life characterized by an irrational response to reality motivated by frustration, fear, and hate.

Jesus was an extremist, although not in terms of the above definition. His extremism was related to love, not hate; faith, not fear; the dignity of man, not his dehumanization. Hence, we are not concerned in this study with the kind of radicalism manifested in the life and teaching of our Lord Jesus Christ.

All that has been said so far about extremists clearly indicates that they are "off center." Polarized on either side of a moderate middle, extremists play their games unbound by the rational rules of society.

Many forms of extremism exist in America: religious, political, and racial. All contribute to the erosion of our democratic way of life. Ultra-ism of various types is poisoning the lifeblood of the nation. To use another figure, ultra-extremists, like tapeworms in the bowels of the body politic, are sapping its energy and making it sick unto death.

Extremism expresses itself in radical rightism and leftism. Astonishing similarities may be seen in the two kinds of extremism. Their familial likeness is inescapable. They are twin brothers whose mother is frustration and whose father is fear. But extremists also manifest basic dissimilarities, as will be seen in the following profiles of the rightist and leftist.

Extremists on the Right

The ultra-rightist betrays a paranoid style of life. A paranoid person is one who is obsessed with the notion that people are plotting against him, persecuting him, even trying to kill him. So it is with the radical rightist. He sees conspiratorial forces directed against him and his country. Communism is the bête noire that threatens him and the world. Aiding and abetting the alleged communist take-over of the country are the Supreme Court, the National Council of Churches, sex education in the public schools, liberal and moderate politicians, fluoridation, welfare programs, and even Santa Claus, who is conceived as a give-away character in a red suit!

THE ANATOMY OF EXTREMISM: RIGHT AND LEFT

Mental health programs by some psychiatrists are seen as a communist weapon to bring about conformity to Marxist ideology.

These and many more individuals and forces are seen as linked together in a gigantic conspiracy to destroy the United States and the free nations of the world. Hence, the rightists stress "law and order" at home and give unqualified support to the war in Vietnam as a means of containing communism abroad.

Radical rightists are angry and tend to locate the cause of their troubles outside themselves. The sources of evil are in society. Hence they project blame upon institutions, persons, and groups which run counter to their prejudices. Scapegoatism is a handy mechanism used to transfer their own guilt to some external object. These extremists are incapable of admitting error and confessing, *Mea culpa*. Consequently, their campaigns are conducted in the spirit of self-righteousness and under the banner of truth and goodness.

Simplistic solutions to complex issues are offered by the rightists. They have plenty of zeal for correcting the evils in society but no working knowledge. Their actions lack the undergirding of sociological and scientific facts. Positive and realistic approaches to the elimination of poverty, racial injustice, blighted urban areas, war, crime, and communism are lacking in their ideology and action.

Superpatriotism is one panacea offered by the radical right for the problems of our nation. It is a narrow, blind patriotism in the mother-God-country syndrome. It is an exaggerated form of nationalism, believing that God is on America's side and that we as a Christian nation must save the world from communism. Acts of intervention in the affairs of other nations, such as Vietnam, are seen to be the will of God for the containment of communism.

The watchword of the superpatriots is "My country, right or wrong." Anyone who does not espouse this provincial brand of patriotism is suspect, perhaps a traitor. To criticize our foreign policy for condoning war and aggression is called unpatriotic. This is the kind of patriotism which Dr. Samuel Johnson called "the last resort of a scoundrel."

There is a place for genuine patriotism in this country. But to be truly patriotic is to express love and loyalty for one's own country and also to be concerned for the welfare of all others. Real patriotism harbors no hatred of other nations but manifests love for all of God's creatures. It does not take satisfaction in the domination of one country over another but seeks the freedom of all.

The rightist often parades under the cloak of religious fundamentalism. Radio preachers who oppose change and social progress receive generous support from those who listen to them. Those cards and letters (with cash) keep coming in. Sermons by these preachers contain little of the gospel but are full of invectives against those who do not agree with their religious and political views.

Ultra-rightist groups use harsh tactics to accomplish their goals. Favorite weapons are rumors, slander, guilt by association, character assassination, disruption of meetings, threatening phone calls, anonymous letters, and violence. Pressures are applied to have subversive teachers fired. Efforts are made to eliminate from the schools books and courses that are allegedly communistic.

Like some communists, some rightists are not averse to use of the big lie. Distortion of the truth is of little significance as long as it helps to defeat the enemy. For example, Carl McIntire, pastor of The Bible Presbyterian Church, president of the American Council of Christian Churches, and radio preacher on "The Twentieth Century Reformation Hour," brands Nels Ferré, a noted theologian, as a blasphemer. He cites in one of Ferré's books the statement that our Lord "must have been born of a German soldier." Book and page number are cited. But a check on the documentation reveals that Nels Ferré does not say this at all. What he does say, on page 191 of *The Christian Understanding of God*, is that such a statement was made by the Nazi propagandist Goebels. But McIntire does not correct this blatant use of the lie to get at another man's reputation. Ferré is the enemy, and any method is justified in destroying him.[5]

A Niagara of noxious literature flows from the rightists to infect the bloodstream of people. Even the sermons of some rightists are filled with invectives, hate, and threats. There is little of the gospel of love and understanding in their messages.

Extremist ideology and extremist action are closely related. The exponents of ultra-ism deny that they use violence or advocate it. Yet they do respond to violence in kind and condone it if it supports their cause. Racial violence is a case in point. Ku Klux Klan leaders denied participating in the bombing of the Baptist church in Birmingham, Alabama, which resulted in the death of four little Negro girls. Yet a Klan leader remarked:

> If they can find those fellows, they ought to pin medals on them. It wasn't no shame they was killed.... Why? Because when I go out to kill rattlesnakes, I don't make no difference between little rattlesnakes and big rattlesnakes.... I say good for whoever planted the bomb.[6]

There is a streak of anti-intellectualism in the ultra-right. Suspicious of "eggheads," rightists tend to respond uncritically to radical reactionaries in the pulpit and in the political arena. Simplistic slogans and solutions to the ills of society are accepted from their leaders as gospel truth. Theirs is a Manichean mentality which sees all issues in black and white. The world is the scene of a conflict between absolute good and evil. Consequently they tolerate no compromises and no ambiguity about right and wrong. Political and social issues are seen as battles between absolute right and absolute wrong, with God on the side of the rightists.

The radical right fears any change in the social status quo. Doubts about any improvement of the present drive them to the past, the good old days of the founding fathers of our country. They have a rear-view mirror

[5] Lewis B. Smedes, "The Gospel According to Carl McIntire," *The Reformed Journal*, January, 1965, p. 17.

[6] "Ku Klux Klans—1965," Anti-Defamation League *Facts*, vol. 16, no. 3 (May, 1965).

perspective on reality, motivated by a fear of losing their sense of security. What they overlook is that the "golden age" of our history was not tranquil and peaceful. Our nation was born in revolution, and many of the founding fathers were revolutionary in their thinking. Thomas Jefferson thought that Shay's Rebellion was a happy thing and that we should have one about every twenty years! In his 1861 inaugural address, Lincoln declared:

> This country, with its institutions, belongs to the people who inhabit it. Whenever they shall grow weary of the existing government they can exercise their constitutional right of amending it, or their revolutionary right to dismember or to overthrow it.

This basic right to change things is clearly articulated in the Declaration of Independence:

> ... Whenever any form of government becomes destructive of these ends [life, liberty, and the pursuit of happiness], it is the right of the people to alter or abolish it, and to institute new government, laying its foundation on such principles and organizing its powers in such a form, as to them shall seem most likely to effect their safety and happiness.

But the rightists quote only those parts of the Constitution, Bill of Rights, and Declaration of Independence which support their rationalized, romantic ideas of a glorious and peaceful past. And they are suspicious of anyone in or out of public office who dares to change things for the greater safety and happiness of all Americans.

Rightists proclaim freedom but deny it to those who do not accept their ideology. By freedom they mean freedom to think and act like the protagonists of the radical right. Recall the 1964 Republican National Convention in San Francisco when some right-wing partisans denied Governor Nelson Rockefeller a chance to be heard. Such acts of radical rightists constitute a flat denial of their professed adherence to the American tradition of freedom.

Rightists are exponents of an ideology of individualism. Individualism is their basic creed. It tends to become absolute, and therefore idolatrous, in the ideology of the rightists. In the realm of economics, individualism is seen as a basic tenet of the Scriptures. It is claimed that uncompromised individualism is the very essence of the gospel. For example, according to the rightists, the free enterprise system rests squarely on the gospel. This stance is taken directly from Adam Smith's *Wealth of Nations*, in which he declares that each person, pursuing his own economic interest, will be led as by a "hidden hand" to produce the greatest good for the greatest number of people. Contrary to the rightists' claims, this is a purely pagan and secular view of economics.

Radical economic individualism rules out a sense of community and a concern for the welfare of others. It rejects one of the basic purposes of the government as indicated in the Constitution: to "promote the general welfare." Economic individualism is insensitive to those who get hurt in the competitive struggle. One of Charles Dickens' characters remarks, "everyone for himself and God for us all, as the elephant said when he danced among the chickens."

Extremists on the Left

Leftism finds expression in numerous organizations and movements in America. Among communist groups may be found the Communist Party, USA (CPA). Founded in Chicago in 1919 as the Communist Labor Party of America, it has changed its name many times, but it remains the orthodox communist party in the nation. In addition, there are the Workers' World Party and other Socialist groups too numerous to mention here. These made up the "Old Left." During the Joseph McCarthy and Eisenhower eras, the Old Left lost much of its thrust and relevance.

The "New Left" of the 1960's was a radical movement discontinuous with the Old Left. The New Left was "born in moral shock," the shock of the awareness of injustice and hypocrisy in American life.[7] According to Jack Newfield, a new leftist, there are approximately 250,000 radical youth in America. Theirs is a heterogeneous movement composed of anarchists, socialists, pacifists, existentialists, transcendentalists, Bohemians, populists, mystics, and black militants.[8]

In the movement are to be found such groups as Trotskyites (Socialist Workers' Party, Spartacists, and Young Socialist Alliance), Maoists (Progressive Labor Movement), W. E. B. Du Bois Clubs, Students for a Democratic Society (SDS), Black Panthers, and the Black Student Union (BSU).

Though at present there are efforts to form a coalition of all the New Left groups, the New Left itself is more a mood than an organization. It has been defined as "an ethical revolt against the visible devils of racism, poverty, war, as well as the less tangible devils of centralized decision-making, manipulative impersonal bureaucracies, and hypocrisies that divide America's ideals from its actions from Watts to Saigon."[9]

For the New Left, the enemy is the Establishment made up of the majority of American people. Specific targets include: the "immoral" and "illegal" war in Vietnam; the military-industrial complex, typified by more than 2000 retired military officers who have connections with the Pentagon and negotiate 90 percent of the contracts for military materials; ROTC (Reserve Officers Training Corps) on college campuses; the Dow Chemical Company, which manufactures napalm and other chemicals used in warfare; racial injustice in both North and South; hypocrisy in politics and international policies; the draft, which discriminates against the poor and the black; universities and colleges, where students have no voice in determining who will teach or what courses will be taught; consensus politics; police brutality; and bureaucratic manipulation.

[7] Michael Novak, *A Theology for Radical Politics* (New York: Herder & Herder, 1969), pp. 31-33.

[8] Jack Newfield, *A Prophetic Minority* (New York: New American Library, 1966), p. 16.

[9] *Ibid.*, p. 15.

THE ANATOMY OF EXTREMISM: RIGHT AND LEFT 19

At present the churches and synagogues have become targets of the radical left. A few years ago James Forman, former leader of the Student Nonviolent Coordinating Committee, and his followers read a "Black Manifesto" to many churches and attempted to take over their denominational headquarters. Forman demanded that churches and synagogues pay five hundred million dollars in reparations to Negroes for the injustices which they have suffered since the time they were first brought to America, and later he raised the demand to three billion dollars.

A profile of the leftists is hard to draw because of the diverse elements in the movement. Yet there are some common traits by which we may identify them.

The new leftists are utopian, idealistic, and sectarian. They envision a new world, a new heaven and a new earth where war, poverty, racial injustice, and other evils do not exist. Revolting against flaws in the American system, they seek a society which will make "love more possible."[10] This boils down to some kind of humanistic and socialistic community, a participatory democracy in which the people decide how they will live and determine their own destiny.

When the structures fail to yield to nonviolent action, the idealistic radical tends to become bitter and disillusioned. He turns to the revolutionary tactics of disruption and violence. Convinced that radical change comes only with violent confrontation, he seeks to destroy the Establishment as the only hope of progress.

There is an authenticity about the leftist in that he rejects the dichotomy between being and act. He is a man of action, and his actions stem not from theory or ideology but from immediate experience. Ideals and actions are inseparable. If there is any theorizing, it grows out of action, not from ideological sources. In short, the leftist carries his ideals to their logical ends in existential action.

Anyone who has witnessed a leftist conference is struck by the fact that these people behave like "self-

[10] *Ibid.*, p. 19.

righteous members of a special sect, confident that their purity of doctrine and purity of life distinguish them from others."[11] Their dogmatism and arrogance equal that of the extreme rightists.

New leftists are appalled by the hypocrisy which prevails in American society. They constantly inveigh against deceit and lying on the part of national leaders. John Foster Dulles, they claim, lied when he declared that the C.I.A. played no role in the 1954 coup in Guatemala; Eisenhower lied about the U-2 flight over the Soviet Union; Adlai Stevenson lied to the United Nations about America's role in the Bay of Pigs invasion; General Westmoreland lied when he declared that we were winning the war in Vietnam. They will not forget that in 1964 Lyndon B. Johnson declared that American boys would not fight on Asian soil battles that Asian boys should fight, nor that by the time he left the White House he had sent 550,000 American boys to Southeast Asia to fight.

New leftists are aware that the older generation professes high ideals but contradicts them in everyday life. A student body president of Colorado University, speaking to the Board of Regents, declared:

> You brought us up to care for our brothers ... not to run away from injustice, but to recognize it and fight it and destroy it. And now you castigate us ... because we think and care.[12]

Leftists reject the past and loathe the present. They are oriented toward the future and deal violently and recklessly with the present. Proud of what they have rejected in the present—middle-class virtues and values, the Establishment—they have only a vague notion of what they really want. No wonder. For a knowledge of the past is essential to know where one has been and necessary in order to know where one is going.

Leftists have a naive view of man. Theirs is a Pelagian position: man is essentially good, and once the social

[11] Novak, *op. cit.*, pp. 50-51.
[12] Louisville *Courier-Journal*, June 8, 1969, p. G-4.

THE ANATOMY OF EXTREMISM: RIGHT AND LEFT 21

order is structured in terms of some form of socialism, the brotherhood of man will prevail. Then, it is alleged, love will be more possible in the world. Such a rosy view of man is the Achilles' heel of all leftist ideology, particularly Marxism. Marxists locate evil primarily in capitalism, which they say must be destroyed before man can be good and just. But man is also evil. Even if a perfect society were possible, man would mar it by manifesting the same old attitudes and traits of aggressiveness and selfishness. Reinhold Niebuhr has realistically observed: "Man's capacity for justice makes democracy possible; but man's inclination to injustice makes democracy necessary."[13]

There is a class consciousness in the New Left. While the new leftists profess to believe that all persons are precious and "beautiful," many of them brand the middle class "slobs" and policemen "pigs."[14] Little place is accorded to reconciliation of the classes in leftist ideology. Hence, leftists are alienating those in the broad middle class, the very people whom they desperately need for their revolution. Some effort is being made to radicalize workers and the professionals, but there will be little success until the new leftists change their disdainful attitudes toward these classes.

"Participatory democracy" is one of the basic principles of the New Left. Yet their members shun the vote process. Both black and white militants ignore "grassroots" democracy. A Louis Harris survey indicates that only 6 percent actually worked for a congressional candidate in 1969, while only 18 percent attended a political rally or heard a candidate speak.[15]

The radical leftist is angry and may resort to the use of violence. Goals are to be achieved by any means possible. Revolutionary rhetoric, vandalism, disruption, personal assault, political guerrilla warfare are legitimate means to ends. Recently the Black Panthers produced a

[13] Reinhold Niebuhr, *The Children of Light and the Children of Darkness* (New York: Scribner's Sons, 1944), p. xi.

[14] Dennis Hale, "The Problem of Ideology," *New Politics*, vol. IV, no. 2, p. 93.

[15] Louisville *Courier-Journal*, March 27, 1969, p. A-11.

coloring book which was distributed to children in elementary schools and urged them to kill policemen. A black militant, lecturing to a class at Southern Baptist Seminary, frankly admitted that he taught his children to kill policemen if attacked by them. He believes that when his children grow up they will do just that.

Leftists hold that they are justified in their use of violence because it is the Establishment which is really violent. The police, the military leaders, the imperialistic capitalists, it is held, are the violent ones in American society. The universities, it is argued, are becoming especially violent institutions, for they train troops in the ROTC, develop chemicals to destroy people and crops, and provide schools of international affairs financed by a "lawless" C.I.A.[16]

Impatient with democratic processes, new leftists demand instant reform (is this the influence of television, where everything is solved in one program?). Like children who want everything now, they lack the patience and discipline of the true revolutionary. Given the conditions in America today with a large middle class and continuous reform, a widespread revolution is not likely in the foreseeable future.

Freedom is a watchword of the New Left. But like the rightists, the leftists are reluctant to grant freedom to those who disagree with them. In the name of freedom, they deprive their fellow students the right to pursue their studies. Guest speakers at universities are yelled down and even assaulted. Nguyen Huu Chi, Ambassador of South Vietnam, was invited to make a speech at New York University. At a given signal members of the SDS climbed up on the stage, physically assaulted the ambassador, and disrupted the meeting. On another floor of the building where James Reston, liberal executive editor of *The New York Times*, was about to speak before an audience of six hundred, the

---

[16] Tariq Ali, ed., *The New Revolutionaries* (New York: William Morrow, 1969), pp. 286-287.

same students battered down the doors and forced the cancellation of the meeting.[17]

Such antics remind us more of storm troopers than of the saviors of our society. Scornful of others who do not agree with them, the leftists are extremely intolerant and totalitarian.

Hatred is a basic virtue of the radical leftists. They denounce American society bitterly and disdainfully and are violently opposed to the capitalistic system. Stokely Carmichael declares that the "young bloods" contain a hatred of which Che Guevara spoke: "Hatred is an element of the struggle . . . relentless hatred of the enemy that impels us over and beyond the natural limitations of man and transforms us into an effective violent, selected and cold killing machine."[18] Carmichael was once asked what he wanted the world to be like and he replied, a world in which "men will love one another."[19] But history proves that such a world can never be built on hatred. To enforce one's will on others by violence, motivated by hatred, is to invite retaliation.

Radical new leftists betray a moral self-righteousness. They pretend that they alone know how to solve the problems of the twentieth century and they alone can be trusted to carry out the solutions. Their protests derive from a Puritan heritage. Satan is incarnate in the Establishment and must be destroyed in the name of righteousness so that people will be saved. Guilt-ridden over our affluency, the war in Vietnam, and racial injustice, they seek to transfer their guilt to someone else. That someone is the college president, the rich man, the conservative politician, or the military leader. If the radical left ever attained power, Puritan tyranny and totalitarianism at its worst would be repeated.

Like the Puritans, new leftists seem to lack a sense of humor and happiness. Little joy is reflected in their

[17] See Sidney Hook, "Who Is Responsible for Campus Violence?", *Saturday Review*, April 19, 1969, pp. 22f.
[18] Ali, *op. cit.*, p. 93.
[19] Novak, *op. cit.*, p. 45.

way of life. Perhaps one of the reasons for this fact is that they are at war within themselves. There is a noticeable amount of self-pity among these young people. In addressing youthful leftists, newspaper writer John Ed. Pearce advises them to leaven their zeal with a little humor, their egotism with a little history; he asks why their insistence on universal love seems so often to express itself in hate for those who differ with them.[20]

As in the case of the rightists, the leftists have their heroes. Among them are Fidel Castro, Che Guevara, Mao Tse-tung, Ho Chi Minh, Malcolm X, and Eldridge Cleaver. Any romantic, guerrilla-style hero fighting the capitalistic system and western society is idolized. Leftist philosophy is eclectic, a conglomeration of ideas from the writings of Jean-Paul Sartre, Albert Camus, Herbert Marcuse, Franz Fanon, and especially Karl Marx. Writings of the New Left are filled with Marxist ideas and terminology. This does not mean that all leftists are communists. While accepting many Marxist-Leninist principles, they reject communist discipline and abhor the thought of being caught up in the party's bureaucracy. Yet the SDS has welcomed communists, and already they are dominating some groups of radical students.

Between the Extremes

Recently an earnest pastor wrote:

> I do not think the extreme John Birch Society or the third-party Wallacites have been able to get through to the people. Somewhere between the polarities of extremism of left and right, I hope to find a workable, acceptable conservatism that will not repel people as fanaticism does.

The problem is to maintain some sort of balance between two extremes. This is a basic issue of our age: how to achieve a balance between freedom for the individual and order in the community. This problem is

---

[20] John Ed. Pearce, "All Right, Youth, Make Something of It," *The Courier-Journal and Times Magazine*, June 16, 1969, p. 27.

illustrated in Schopenhauer's parable of the porcupines. On a cold, wintry night a group of porcupines were confronted with the problem of how to keep far enough apart from each other to prevent sticking each other to death and yet close enough together to keep from freezing to death.

If such a balance is to be achieved, it will be by a creative political center. Centrists know that it is not an easy matter to occupy the *via media* between two extremes. As the late President Dwight D. Eisenhower remarked: "It often takes more courage to occupy the center than any other position in the political arena, for you are then subject to attack on *both* flanks."[21]

A truly creative center will have a clear and cogent political philosophy in a pluralistic society. It will embrace some of the aspirations and hopes of all the people. It will overcome the contradiction between our professed ideals of "liberty and justice for all" and the denial of these in practice. As a government of the people, by the people, and for the people, the creative center will combine both the cherished American traditions of the conservatives and the aspirations of the liberals for reform. Such a society may be called "a democracy in a republic."

In a creative center, change would be achieved through democratic means. Since we have constitutional and legal means for changing governmental policies in the United States, revolutionary violence is not defensible. Moreover, violence has never been very effective in securing massive reforms in a democratic society where there are legal means of changing things.

But extremists will insist that to follow the snail-like pace of reform in keeping with constitutional principles is ineffective and results in a mediocre, passive middle. Hence, while demanding their constitutional rights, they deny others these same rights. They turn the liberty of the First Amendment into license. Freedom of speech and freedom of the press are guaranteed to all citizens,

[21] Dwight D. Eisenhower, "We *Must* Avoid the Perils of Extremism," *The Reader's Digest*, April, 1969, p. 105.

but no one has the freedom to abuse others or to destroy private and public property. The First Amendment insures the right of assembly, but it must be peaceable assembly.[22]

Civil disobedience is a cherished American principle that is often debased by extremists. Some of them break the law while demonstrating and then demand amnesty. But civil disobedience requires that one accept the consequences of one's actions and avoid hurting others. John Bunyan, Mahatma Gandhi, Henry David Thoreau, and Martin Luther King, Jr., expected to suffer the consequences of their conduct. They were fully responsible for their acts. But extremists want to have their cake and eat it too. If they were really sincere, they would accept their punishment when they use civil disobedience as an instrument for their cause. To refuse to do so is to degrade a basic principle of freedom and an effective means of social reform in a democratic society.

Much of our tension and many of our social issues could be resolved by a more imaginative and aggressive political center. Too many people in the center withdraw from existential involvement in the political arena. To be indifferent to political participation in a democratic society is to be irresponsible. The ancient Greeks had a word for the citizen who dissociates himself from civic responsibility. The word was *idiotes*, from which we get the English word "idiot." Originally the term meant anyone who neglected his public duties and led a private, selfish existence.[23]

It is imperative that citizens at the center work enthusiastically and courageously for the extension of democratic principles and their application to all American citizens. This would have the effect of taking the steam out of the fanatics on the fringes who capitalize on the problems of war, poverty, political sham, racial injustice, and hypocrisy.

[22] Abe Fortas, *Concerning Dissent and Civil Disobedience* (New York: New American Library, 1968), p. 34.

[23] J. T. Shipley, *Dictionary of Word Origins* (Patterson, N. J.: Littlefield, Adams, 1964), p. 186.

A creative center would rearrange our priorities so as to achieve a more humanized society. The energy and skill expended to place man on the moon must be turned to the less glamorous problems on earth. The billions of dollars spent on weapons of destruction must be used to develop instruments for human welfare. Billions spent for the manufacture of poisonous gases must be applied to the eradication of the ear, eye, nose, and throat pollution which is destroying our mental and physical health. In short, national priorities must be changed to meet basic human needs with better health, housing, and education for all citizens of this country.

We do not need to junk our present system of government as the radicals advocate. Our government is still robust and strong despite many minor ailments. But progress toward a healthier body politic must be escalated. We are moving in the right direction, though at glacial speed. The question is whether we will move far enough fast enough.

Unless Americans who stand for peace and progress through democratic means enter more vigorously into the struggle for a more just society, the extremists will continue to flourish in our nation. If the majority of American citizens assume an Olympian aloofness from the struggle for humanization of all classes of citizens, extremists may eventually destroy the basic principles that have made this nation great.

2
Common Features of Extremism's Ugly Faces

H. Clayton Waddell

Strong differences of opinion have always been a feature of the American scene. Democracy invites and approves conflicting ideas—indeed must have them, for it is out of conflict that consensus is achieved. Still,

> the Judeo-Christian tradition demands that conflict be rooted in reason and in truth and in charity, not in hysteria and in falsehood and in hate. Herein rests the basic difficulty with both the Communist Left and the Radical Right. [1]

Extremist upsurges have dotted the history of this country since it first began to flex its muscles. The forces that ignite them are usually latent but never dead. Although waves of extremism are not all cut from one pattern, they do have common distinguishing elements. In the effort to characterize and classify extremist groups they are labeled "right" and "left," or more precisely "far right" and "far left." This designation calls up the visual image of opposite ends of a straight

---

[1] Ralph Lord Roy, "Conflict from the Communist Left and the Radical Right," in *Religion and Social Conflict*, Robert Lee and Martin E. Marty, ed. (New York: Oxford University Press, 1964), p. 68.

H. Clayton Waddell is Professor of Social Ethics, New Orleans Baptist Theological Seminary, New Orleans, Louisiana.

line. Examination of the two groups, however, leads to the conclusion that they are more like broken ends of a fractured circle, quite close together. It is the purpose of this paper to explore some of the ways in which the right and the left resemble each other, particularly in ruling out reason, truth, and charity.

The left today ranges from Trotskyites to Maoists and from bearded anti-war protesters to barefoot poverty workers and militant students. For clarity and brevity and in order to narrow a wide and scattered field, this paper will deal with the American Communist Party and groups or individuals purposefully and intentionally sympathetic to that party as the common denominator of the left. By the right or the right wing we will mean that loose configuration of organizations and individuals, under no one leader and following no definitive party line but still a cohesive and visible group.

Effort will be made at all times to draw a line between responsible conservatism and the radical right wing. It might be helpful to state as an operating premise that

> the difference lies basically in two broad areas, namely, their conceptions of the nature of the communist conspiracy and their approaches to achieving their aims. Radical Rightists are convinced of the absoluteness of the communist menace. Everything in the world is seen in terms of the life and death struggle between "slavery" and "freedom," and the communists are winning because they recognize the true nature of the contest. Implicit in this is the idea of conspiracy. Communism is primarily an internal threat because its adherents are seeking to gain control of the institutions of government, education, and religion. Rightists believe in gigantic "control apparatus" in the government which is endeavoring to transform the country into a "collectivist" state by gradual encroachment in the economic sphere and to destroy the old-fashioned American belief in Christianity and rugged individualism.[2]

---

[2] Richard V. Pierard, "Christianity, Democracy, and the Radical Right," in *Protest and Politics*, Robert G. Clouse, Robert D. Linder, and Richard V. Pierard, ed. (Greenwood, S. C.: Attic Press, 1968), pp. 39-40.

It is the thesis of the contemporary radical right that when the time is ripe (and that time is imminent) "the Soviet Union will move in, take over the United States, and complete the task of enslaving the American population."[3]

The responsible conservative may deplore the decline of traditional values and may differ politically from those who seem to him to dominate the country, but he is willing to follow the methods and operate through the channels of democratic government to bring about change. "He is willing to endure the compromise . . . the continuous give and take necessary for change without chaos. This is an outstanding feature of the American genius, never fully understood by foreigners or by native extremists."[4]

Although extremists on the left and the right may refuse to "claim kin," examination of the record shows that they are sometimes blood brothers. This discussion will be limited to the following rather obvious ways in which they are related: First, both extremes distrust the democratic process. Second, both oversimplify problems, issues, and solutions. Third, both look upon those who disagree with or oppose them as members of a conspiracy. Fourth, both distrust any instrument of international cooperation. And both the left and the right, finally, consider people to be expendable.

Extremists Distrust the Democratic Process

Seymour Martin Lipset once observed:

> In a real sense, extremists of the right and left have in common much more than they would have us believe. Each of them deliberately sets out to destroy the underlying base of a democratic social order, that is they destroy confidence in government and its functions.[5]

[3] *Ibid.*, p. 40.
[4] George B. Leonard, "What Is an Extremist?", *Look*, October 20, 1964, pp. 36-37.
[5] Seymour Martin Lipset, "The Sources of the 'Radical Right,'" in *The Radical Right* (Garden City, N. Y.: Doubleday, 1963), pp. 311-312.

COMMON FEATURES OF EXTREMISM'S UGLY FACES

The Communist Party is an open threat to American democracy. It avowedly seeks to undermine the basis of civil liberties and boasts of the coercive measures it has brought to bear upon the democratic processes in the U.S.A. It makes no attempt to hide the fact that its purpose is to undermine confidence in our democratic underpinnings. The right-wing extremist, on the other hand, destroys democracy while pretending to defend it. Henry Steele Commager states it thus:

> Those who cultivate and spread the gospel of hatred throughout our society bear a heavy responsibility. They do not really weaken Communism; they weaken democracy and liberty. By their conduct and their philosophy they lower the moral standards of the society they pretend to defend. Eager to put down imagined subversion, they are themselves the most subversive of all the elements of our society.[6]

There is no doubt that many earnest people who think they are helping to destroy the dragons that threaten our country are helping to destroy the country instead.

While it would be irresponsible to minimize the magnitude of the danger that worldwide communism poses for free America, it is more irresponsible so to distort the image of that danger that the real hazard is clouded over, even lost sight of. Right-wing extremists have irresponsibly used the weapons of hate, suspicion, distrust, and fear to turn man against man and destroy the confidence of the American people in their chosen leaders and their institutions. Using innuendo and guilt by association, they have fragmented communities and done violence to innocent citizens. While it is not within the scope of this paper to probe into the causes of this ugly phenomenon, it might be suggested in passing that

> we could take a leaf from a physics text and propose a law of diminishing reason: man's capacity to act sensibly, in the face of danger, varies inversely with the magnitude of the danger. The greater the danger, the greater the tendency toward irrational frenzy. Whether a person understands the

[6] Henry Steele Commager, "A Historian Looks at Our Political Morality," *Saturday Review*, July 10, 1965, p. 18.

danger, and whether he is prepared for it, also affects his judgment. But even so, our wits suffer the most strain exactly when most needed.[7]

Freedom is the lifeblood of the American nation. America was conceived in freedom. America was born in freedom. America is nurtured in freedom. The Declaration of Independence and the Constitution of the United States are documents designed to define and perpetuate a free life for a free people. Ours must remain a government "of the people, by the people, and for the people," for it is within the framework of our democratic, constitutional form of government that our lives are ordered and we are able to breathe free air. Democracy is the bedrock of our nation and its institutions. Yet in the name of Americanism the right-wing extremists, calling themselves patriots, deliberately endeavor to undermine the faith of the American people in our democratic form of government and the democratic process. They disregard the "procedures of a free society: the ballot, the lawsuit, the strike, the petition, complaints to the press, action through established grievance procedures."[8]

The democratic process lives or dies with rational debate and constructive argument. In the closed systems of the extremist camps, both left and right, debate is impossible. Extremism cannot tolerate diversity, which is the lifeblood of democracy and freedom. Only the predetermined, one-sided approach dictated by the system is tolerated. Facts are interpreted and shaped to fit conclusions already drawn. The give-and-take of political argument is ruled out. There must be no difference of opinion from that which is handed down from the top. What the individual thinks or feels does

[7] Gordon L. Shull, "Communism and Anti-Communism in America: The Long Road to Reason," *Social Progress* (United Presbyterian Church in the U.S.A.), November-December, 1966, p. 11.

[8] John W. Gardner, Godkin Lectures at Harvard University, March, 1969, quoted in *Christian Science Monitor*, April 16, 1969, p. 10.

not matter, and there is no room for collective and democratic decision-making.

The two-party system that has characterized the American political system has a built-in, creative opposition. But to the superpatriot, the critic becomes the villain and coercion takes the place of persuasion. Both the right and the left think they alone know the infallible truth. The courts are not allowed to speak against them. Even the Supreme Court comes to be considered an agent of the enemy and should be dissolved.

The keynote of right-wing extremist thinking, like that of the communist, is distrust of democracy. Those who will listen are fed a diet of propaganda of which the following is typical. In the words of the extremist author, vast numbers of Americans are awakening

> to the dangers of a democracy, to the fact that our Founding Fathers themselves ... feared a democracy as the worst of all forms of government, and to what our Supreme Court was doing to convert our constitutional republic into a democracy as a help to the Communists.[9]

Senator Stephen Young of Ohio once said of contemporary right-wing extremists, "These groups undermine our basic institutions and try to reshape America into a totalitarian-fascist state."[10] Another writer once commented in a similar situation, "Open fascism they recognized, but not the fascist sword of the bourgeoisie concealed in the scabbard of democracy."[11]

Extremists Oversimplify Complex Problems

"All extremists," said one writer, "are somehow the same. All share one crucial goal: a desire to 'go back.' "[12]

---

[9] Robert Welch, *Bulletin*, July, 1964.

[10] "Danger on the Right," *Saturday Evening Post*, January 6, 1962, p. 6.

[11] Daniel Aaron, *Writers on the Left: Episodes in American Literary Communism* (New York: Harcourt, Brace & World, 1961), p. 378.

[12] Leonard, *loc. cit.*

Nostalgia makes us all look backward at times. The extremist sees a literal going back as the answer to all the complex problems that beset today's world. He longs for the private and the familiar experiences of yesterday and the security that once enveloped him. Instead of trying to cope with a world he does not understand he proposes to abandon it. The writer just quoted adds:

> The American Communist longs for a lost time when issues were simple—when, as Marx wrote, the worker was always oppressed, always pure; when the Capitalist was always the oppressor, always evil. Like all extremists, the Communist seeks simplicity. The many shades of gray in our complex, well-to-do, middle-class society dazzle him.
>
> The Muslim or Black Nationalist, like his Ku Klux Klan counterpart, wants to return to total segregation. He wants to go back—as far as Africa. He cannot cope with the painful adjustments on the road to integration ....
>
> The Far-Right extremist dreams of the dear, dead days of the 1890's, when life was straight and simple (or so his nostalgia tells him). He holds that such annoying complexities as urbanization, social security, international relations, the United Nations and the income tax can be banished by a wave of the American flag.[13]

Another commentator made the statement that the extremists reject "the whole present—not merely that part of the present which all sensible men would like to reject."[14]

Radicals read history, but they do not like it. They would like to repeal the twentieth century and return to an idealized, individualistic rural society where they could control their future.

In the attacks upon communism by the right and upon capitalistic imperialism by the left, life takes on meaning and purpose. The extremists have a sense of participating in decisions of vital public concern. They have found in this device a simple means of working for their Utopia. Their rigid systems make it necessary that

[13] *Ibid.*
[14] William S. White, "The New Irresponsibles," *Harper's*, November, 1961, pp. 98-108.

they maintain a stereotyped view of communism on the one hand and capitalism on the other. Such closed systems do not allow for doubt or testing. Every situation is seen as black or white, good or bad, war or peace. This kind of simplification enables the extremists to deal with complex problems by simply ignoring the complicating factors. Leaders of the right have made naive statements such as: "The Cuban problem could be settled by applying the Monroe Doctrine." "We could have stopped the Berlin Wall by closing the Russian Embassy in Washington." "World communism would collapse if we would stop helping the communists."

The simplistic approach to many-faceted problems is seen in the current outcry for "law and order." The communists, no doubt, felt very good when in the course of the recent presidential campaign "George Wallace announced that, if necessary, he would establish 'law and order' by stationing soldiers with fixed bayonets every few feet on our city streets."[15] Oversimplified solutions to vastly complex problems are at best naive, at worst very dangerous. One wise man has advised that we had better learn to cope with this strange new universe if we wish to escape the fate of the dinosaur.

Any Opposition Is Seen as a Conspiracy

The extreme right and the extreme left are dependent upon each other for survival. Communism and capitalism are both seen by their enemies to be conspiracies, and without each other their cause for being would vanish.

> According to the neo-Stalinist wing in Russia today, almost all intellectuals and reformers are secret agents of western capitalism. According to the right wing today in America, almost all intellectuals and reformers are secret agents of eastern Communism. Mirror images, of course. And wrong twice.
>
> Each mirror image needs the other and reflects on the

[15] Peter Berger, "Between Tyranny and Chaos," *The Christian Century*, October 30, 1968.

other. They need each other as bogeymen. They reflect on each other because each leftist extreme frightens waverers into the rightist camp; each rightist extreme frightens waverers into the leftist camp. McCarthyism used to frighten European liberals into being fellow-travelers with communism. Communism frightens American conservatives into being fellow-travelers with pseudo-conservative nationalist thought controllers.[16]

During the 1940's the pro-communists in our country saw their hopes for a perfect world shattered and suspected a fascist conspiracy within the United States.

> The danger was basically *internal.* "Nazis are running the American government," Henry Wallace declared at one passionate moment in 1948. Our two major parties had "rotted," and Wall Street, the military clique, labor "misleaders," "red-baiting" intellectuals, and even the churches had become part of the program to "betray" peace and progress. Unless "the people" rose and shook off this conspiracy, the left warned, the country faced an imminent Fascist takeover, and American foreign policy would serve only dictator regimes and the former Fascist nations.[17]

This is a close parallel to the conspiracy theory which the extreme right espouses today. The *Blue Book* of the John Birch Society tells us, "Highly placed secret Communists, or at least workers for the Communist cause, is something with which we are absolutely loaded." We are solemnly warned that the Communist advance has already gone very far indeed and that there is imminent and horrible "danger of the physical enslavement of the whole world."[18]

The right wing sees the communist infiltration of America as a massive internal conspiracy, dedicated to the destruction of everything the American people hold dear. The communists are believed to hold the reins of history in their hands, and at the proper moment they will change its course to suit their whims and evil

[16] "The Philosophical 'New Conservatism,'" *The Radical Right*, pp. 172-173.

[17] Alan F. Westin, "The John Birch Society—1962," *The Radical Right*, p. 219.

[18] *The Blue Book of the John Birch Society*, p. 71.

desires. Their demonic power is a threat that must be confronted immediately and at all costs.

Once it is accepted that our government is permeated by communism and that trusted leaders are traitors, the rest of the phantasmagoria follows. The person who is already overcome by fears often gives in to the harangues of extremist demagogues and joins the all-out campaign to eliminate the satanic menace. Emotions are exploited for all they are worth. The "Grand Wizard" of the Ku Klux Klan has said: "The Klan does not believe that the fact that it is emotional and instinctive, rather than coldly intellectual, is a weakness. All action comes from emotion, rather than from ratiocination."[19] Working upon this conviction, extremist leaders freely resort to misrepresentation, subversion, innuendo, and the Big Lie. Their overwrought followers are incited to hysterical, irrational, even violent action. "Bodily harm and arson or, in the case of the McCarthy paroxysm, character assassination constituted their notion of serving the public good, instead of the slow and (to them) highly suspect workings of the law."[20]

The Joe McCarthy episode serves as a good example of what can happen when extremist groups make irresponsible, venomous attacks on individuals, institutions, and organizations whose chief sin is disagreement with the group's ideology. Rumor and guilt by association are deadly weapons of the extremists. Perhaps they take a cue from Shakespeare's lines in Henry IV, Part II:

> Rumor is a pipe
> Blown by surmises, jealousies, conjectures,
> And of so easy and so plain a stop
> That the blunt monster with uncounted heads,
> The still-discordant wavering multitude,
> Can play upon it!

Wild charges of "conspiracy" have swept across the nation in this decade. Extremists saw the fluoridation of city water as a communist plot to soften the brains of

[19] Arthur M. Schlesinger, Sr., "Extremism in American Politics," *Saturday Review,* November 27, 1965, p. 24.
[20] *Ibid.*

Americans to make them easier to brainwash with communist propaganda. Their

> ... attack on mental health was first set off by the passage of a perfectly innocent bill by Congress in 1956 to finance the construction and operation of a mental hospital in Alaska. The extremists concluded that this was "a plot to establish a concentration camp for political opponents of the Eisenhower Administration! ... A ruse to kidnap anti-Communists."[21]

More recent is the charge that sex education in the public schools is something dreamed up by the communists to corrupt our youth and drag them into the communist fold. On July 10, 1969, the following appeared in the *Nashville Tennessean:*

> With the public schools closed for the summer, the controversy over sex education has temporarily subsided, but only on the surface. All signs point to a renewed and enlarged fight in the fall, for it is increasingly clear that much of the protest is not spontaneous, but inspired by organized agitation. There no longer is any doubt that the protest campaign has a rightwing, fundamentalist, anti-communist flavor.... There is a national pattern and an underlying theme to the resistance movement, which has been pointedly expressed by Robert Welch, founder and leader of the John Birch Society. Sex education, he says, is "a filthy communist plot."

Both Left and Right Distrust International Cooperation

Extremists agree in their opposition to the international instruments which nations are struggling to fashion to promote peace and prevent nuclear war. The right wing sees international cooperation as a communist conspiracy designed to soften America for communist domination. The communists see international organizations as instruments of capitalistic imperialism designed to stop the spread of communism. The right wants to destroy the United Nations as an instrument of peaceful coexistence. The communists would keep the

---

[21] Donald Robinson, "Conspiracy USA," *Look*, January 26, 1965, p. 32.

United Nations but would hamper its effectiveness except when cooperation would be to the communist advantage.

Both the right and the left are against foreign aid: the right because it would help the communist conspiracy and the left because it would help end the poverty, ignorance, and disease which condition people for communist inroads.

Instead of arbitration, the extremists put their confidence in force. This was demonstrated by the invasion of Czechoslovakia by troops from the Soviet Union. Closer to home, the extreme right clamors for "no appeasement" in Vietnam, and with their "better dead than red" philosophy they see no obstacle to the use of nuclear weapons. Their leaders would have us wage preemptive war while there is still an "advantage over the enemy." Force remains the one method expected to be effective in the showdown—against fascism by the communist and against communism by the extreme right.

Neither the right nor the left has any scruples about how they acquire power. Any method that works is condoned. The right is likely to equate power with military victory, and they go on the theory that there is no substitute for victory. Their formula for international relations is likely to be reduced to some such simple equation as: "Invade Cuba." "Knock down the Berlin Wall." "Turn the Vietnam War over to the military." "Destroy the enemy in order to save him." "We must stop the enemy in Saigon or fight him in California." The left is willing to resort to the most radical methods to subdue restive people when they deem it advisable.

Since the right wing is so controlled by the ideology of a massive internal communist conspiracy, it fails to see the real threat of international communism and discredits the agencies and programs which provide a necessary shield for peace and freedom against aggression. The communists are happy to see the extremists of the right agitating for the elimination of regional organizations such as the North Atlantic Treaty Organization (NATO) and the South East Asia Treaty Organization (SEATO). The more isolationist the United States becomes, the easier it will be for the communists to win in the world. When anticommunists concentrate on removing books from library shelves, reducing foreign aid to needy countries, and undermining the democratic way of life in America, the communists rejoice. In every such instance the right wing is working for them, doing the things they could not do for themselves.

Both Right and Left See People as Expendable

The right and the left both hope to control the future of America, and both are willing to use people as pawns in their struggle for power. Both strive to dominate the thought processes of the American masses and care little about the individual. "Fear is essential to the salvation of the American republic," says Clarence Manion, one of the strident voices of the right.[22] Thus the hucksters of hysteria play upon the emotions of the people to arouse fear, hostility, suspicion, anger, and alarm. When these emotions are fully aroused the people are ready for appropriate doses of an extremist doctrine.

Extremists saturate the people with a distorted picture of the nature of a problem. Facts are sifted and always interpreted to fit the listener of the moment. The purpose of the propaganda is to create revolutionary situations in which an organized, single-minded minority can seize power. Facts are hidden and the public is bombarded with false information. Fair and free competition with another system of thought has no place in the thinking of the extremist. Social engineering, manipulation of one's fellow man, is simply the means to a necessary end.

The left is constantly on the alert for discontent, injustice, or the misuse of power in the social arena. It is ready to exploit any such opportunity for propaganda.

> Communists usually offer one aspect of their teachings to a group or an individual—that aspect which appeals to

[22] Gordon W. Allport, "The Religious Context of Prejudice," *Information Service*, April 22, 1967, p. 7.

the interests of the groups or the temperament of the individual in question: to the underprivileged masses, it is equality and security and what they call economic justice ... to soft pacifists, it is attacks against warmongers and petitions for world peace, ... to the liberals it is what they call the struggle against fascism. Now so far as they go, these partial emphases of Communism have each a germ of truth. But they are not the whole truth about Communism. They are not the essence of Communism. Nor can the abstract good in them stand up, white and radiant, outside the dark shadow of the whole system.[23]

The various aspects of communist dogma are used as bait to capture a willing disciple. Afterward the moment of truth may dawn.

Both the right and the left are self-appointed champions of the cause of freedom, but they fail to acknowledge that freedom and responsibility go together. They overlook the obvious fact that in order for a man to be free he must participate in the decisions that govern his life. Decisions in extremist groups are made from above, and woe to him who deviates from the established doctrine. He is castigated as an enemy of the cause and faces appropriate punitive action. Any dissent is seen as treason. John W. Gardner has warned, "The debasement of the critical makes responsible action for social change increasingly difficult."[24]

The right-wing peddlers of propaganda, halftruths, and outright lies perform their dismal tasks in the name of patriotism. In the name of democracy they destroy the foundations of democracy and undermine men's confidence in basic institutions, including the church. "In the name of freedom [they] stab freedom in the dark; in the name of Christianity ... [they] use the weapons of the devil."[25] With their tarbrush techniques, the extremists of the right mount their soap boxes and proclaim to the credulous that even many of

[23] Charles Malik, "Communism," *The Christian Century*, January 17, 1951.

[24] Gardner, *loc. cit.*

[25] Schlesinger, *op. cit.*, p. 23.

our presidents have been the unwitting dupes of the communist conspiracy. They solemnly point out that "Judaism" and the civil rights movement are communist conspiracies calculated to wreck the nation. They fill the air waves with charges that the churches, Protestant and Catholic alike, are deeply infiltrated by communists.

An ugly part in this unlovely drama is that played by the extremist who exploits well-meaning fellow citizens for profit. One well-informed writer has warned that we "ought never to confuse genuine American anti-Communism ... with the pseudo-anti-Communism of the demagogues, which is not anti-Communism at all but a racket."[26] These extremists fan emotional flames to fatten their own purses. A national information service has noted,

> When Dan Smoot took to denouncing integration as "An American Tragedy" created by communist infiltration of the South, *The Dallas News* attacked "the professionals for profit who have found a remunerative field" in opposition to Communism. "Patriotism is a justly venerated human quality," editorialized the *News*. "Patriotism for profit is justly suspect.... If Mr. Smoot has not been around long enough to encounter it the *News* has. When your daily mail includes such tripe as defining communism as a Jewish conspiracy, a Catholic conspiracy, and an NAACP conspiracy, you can discern the hand of the patrioteer for profit.... The ... question is whether a man is out to make a fast buck or to serve the community."[27]

People are not, under any circumstances, to be used or exploited. If this does happen the nation is robbed of its greatest potential. The freedom of the people must be protected with the utmost care in order that each person may become a responsible citizen.

In conclusion we could do no better than to quote the admonition of President Lyndon B. Johnson in his first address to Congress:

---

[26] Peter Viereck, "The Revolt Against the Elite—1955," *The Radical Right*, p. 142.

[27] Allport, *op. cit.*, p. 8.

Let us put an end to the teaching and preaching of hate and evil and violence. Let us turn away from the fanatics of the far left and the far right, from the apostles of bitterness and bigotry, from those defiant of law, and those who pour venom into our Nation's blood stream.[28]

[28] *Congressional Record*, 88th Congress, First Session, 1963, CIX, Part 17, p. 22839.

3
Who's Who Among the Extremists

G. Willis Bennett

No one can deal adequately and responsibly with the topic of extremism without sooner or later making an effort to identify and characterize various groups and persons that commonly are so classified. It is a risky task. Wayne E. Oates suggests that to talk about groups being extreme is to outline one's own shadow.[1] We tell others as much about ourselves, he says, as we tell them about extremism. Nevertheless, if the topic is to be treated in more than a general way, one needs some illustrations. It is not with any ill intent that I therefore engage in the process of identification. I include only groups or persons commonly identified as extremists by reliable research authorities today. While I have known some members of extremist groups and have talked with them to learn their philosophy and goals, my knowledge of extremism is chiefly based not upon first-hand knowledge but upon research. The process of identifying groups and persons as extremists on the right and left has been pursued by others, and I pass on their findings. We make this effort to identify and study objectively in

[1] Wayne E. Oates, *Pastoral Counseling in Social Problems: Extremism, Race, Sex, Divorce* (Philadelphia: Westminster Press, 1966), p. 37.

G. Willis Bennett is Associate Professor of Christian Ethics, Southern Baptist Theological Seminary, Louisville, Kentucky.

order that we may better understand these movements—their mood, their philosophy, their goals—and therefore better understand the threat to human freedom, the social order, and the free exercise of religion.

Sorting Out the Left

Communist Party USA. Any treatment of the left ought perhaps to begin with the Communist Party USA. A good treatment of communism and some of the implications for our nation today is Henlee Barnette's book, *Communism: Who? What? Why?*[2] Between the 1930's and 1950 the party saw its maximum growth in America. Its membership, at least its known membership, declined greatly during the Joseph McCarthy period. During the fifties, members of the party were in the courts, in jail under the Smith Act, and on the boat back to Europe under the McCarran Immigration Act. The remnant went underground or out of the party. In the early sixties the party saw a revival in America. More favorable court decisions struck down repressive legislation, and certain controversial actions of the government such as those at the Bay of Pigs, the Dominican Republic, and Vietnam contributed to the growth of the American left. In 1966 the party held a five-day convention, the first open to the press.[3] These original left-wing extremists were being called old fogies and they didn't like it. Leader Gus Hall boasted of past successes in a report that lasted three hours. He argued that the New Left would find that the CPA was relevant. Indeed, the party is estimated to have doubled its membership in the sixties[4] and was strong enough to conduct a Spring Mobilization against the war in 1968, to sponsor an October Stop the Draft Week, and to make a major impact upon some groups of the New Left. Michael Miles in an article about "The Communist Party Today"

[2] Nashville, Tennessee: Broadman Press, 1962.
[3] Myron Feinsilber, "Communists in Convention," *Commonweal*, July 22, 1966, p. 464.
[4] Michael Miles, "The Communist Party Today," *The New Republic*, February 3, 1968, p. 22.

declares that the New Left "has been coming around to Marxism," and there is some evidence to justify his conclusion.[5]

The New Left. Probably the most controversial radical movement in America is that known as the New Left, and several groups in it will now claim our attention.

The New Left is composed of black, white, and racially mixed groups. The common denominator among them seems to be protest, rebellion, and sometimes anarchy. Common concerns include the war and the draft; civil rights and the elimination of poverty; and rejection of authority and the Establishment, either on or off campus. The Old Left has played its part in organizing and motivating the nation toward the welfare state, but the New Left has rebelled against benevolent Big Brother. Paul Jacobs, an Old Leftist, has said, "We were rejecting a depression; they're rejecting affluence."[6] Sociologist Daniel Bell concludes: "At best, the New Left is all heart. At worst, it is no mind."[7]

Whatever one thinks of the New Left, it is evident that these radicals, some but not all of whom would be called extremists, have changed the temper, the tone, and the terms of American politics. They are mostly young, bright, and middle class, coming from highly respected families. They sometimes act as if they have no memory and have read no history. Jack Newfield in his book, *A Prophetic Minority*, tends to disclaim this conclusion, however.[8] He claims that it is because many of the young idealists among the New Left have read history and do have memories that they react against the Establishment and the hypocrisy of middle-class America. The extremists among the New Left would destroy the status quo now and worry about rebuilding later. Not all groups feel this way, and some that now advance such a philosophy did not start out that way.

[5] *Ibid.*, p. 25.
[6] "The New Radicals," *Time*, April 28, 1967.
[7] *Ibid.*
[8] Jack Newfield, *A Prophetic Minority* (New York: Signet Books, 1967).

Several New Left groups began with idealism, worthy and honorable goals, and acceptable though aggressive methodology. It was the reaction to them and their goals, the opposition and sometimes violence they received from the Establishment, that led them to a counter reaction that resulted in greater hostility, a change in methodology, and a type of revolutionary action. Many persons who do not endorse the violence and anarchy of the movement would agree with a *Time* magazine editorial: "There should always be a New Left—to drive conventional society to a constant, sometimes painful review of its own values."[9]

Let us look at several groups which have been a part of the movement.

Student National Coordinating Committee (SNCC) was originally formed in 1960 in Atlanta, Georgia, as the Student Nonviolent Coordinating Committee. A founding statement of purpose adopted by the 235 intelligent, well-dressed, middle-class students shows the high idealism of its beginning. It reads in part:

> We affirm the philosophical or religious ideal of non-violence as the foundation of our purpose, the presupposition of our belief, and the manner of our action.
>
> Non-violence, as it grows from the Judeo-Christian tradition, seeks a social order of justice permeated by love. Integration of human endeavor represents the crucial first step toward such a society.
>
> Through non-violence, courage displaces fear. Love transcends hate. Acceptance dissipates prejudice, hope ends despair. Faith reconciles doubt. Peace dominates war. Mutual regards cancel enmity. Justice for all overthrows injustice. The redemptive community supersedes immoral social systems.[10]

Once the nonviolence of SNCC got underway, it was greeted by bombs in Georgia, brutality in Alabama, and murder in Mississippi. Civil rights were not to be given to Negroes without much resistance, and social change was not to come without bloodshed. As time wore on

---

[9] "The New Radicals," *Time*, April 28, 1967.
[10] Newfield, *op. cit.*, p. 47.

the ideals expressed in the statement began to be replaced with words that spoke of power, politics, and pressure. In the annual meeting of SNCC in 1966, John Lewis, who held out for nonviolent methods, was reelected to his leadership role. But before the heated debates of the week were over it became evident that the group was preparing for a more militant stance. They reversed their earlier decision and replaced Lewis with Stokely Carmichael; basically they adopted the goal of gaining black power through violence. After the stormy actions of the next several months, H. Rap Brown replaced Carmichael. Its philosophy and methodology greatly changed, SNCC lost many members to other movements and has declined in influence. The name change which dropped "Nonviolent" and added "National" to the name of this organization reflects its present strategy to promote guerrilla warfare training in urban areas throughout the nation.[11]

Students for a Democratic Society (SDS) was founded in Michigan in June, 1962, by fifty-five youths from eleven colleges. Later the headquarters were moved to Chicago and SDS became the chief instrument for campus rebellions, riots, strikes, and take-overs. SDS began, as Paul Booth described it, as an effort to open a dialogue with the liberals, to organize the grassroots, and to aid in bringing about social change. By 1965, when Booth spoke to the National Press Club, few could find fault with SDS's idealism or with the commitment demonstrated by many of the youth who gave up affluence for service, success for danger, and comfort for sacrifice and even death. Many of them proved themselves in the Peace Corps, the Job Corps, and VISTA. Many lived in American slums on ten dollars a week and identified with the poor whose interest they sought to serve.

Frustration and despair, resulting from progress that was too slow and criticism that was frequently unjust, led to a changed philosophy on the part of some mem-

---

[11] J. Edgar Hoover, *Testimony Before Senate Subcommittee on Appropriations,* June 24, 1971, p. 76.

bers of SDS. Some of their leaders denounced the United States as a "capitalist, imperialist, racist" state, and they proposed to "destroy the ruling class" and "build a Marxist-Leninist revolutionary movement."[12]

Differences within the SDS resulted in a split into three groups with a combined membership of about 2500. The groups are the Worker Student Alliance (WSA); the Revolutionary Youth Movement; and a number of unaffiliated chapters. The WSA has become the principal SDS chapter. It is controlled by the pro-Chinese Communist Progressive Labor Party.[13]

The *Weatherman* organization, which has disassociated itself from the SDS to practice more violent tactics, is a paramilitary group, seeking to bring about revolution through urban guerrilla warfare. Its members (probably about 1500) have declared war on their enemies within the country and have taken credit for a number of bombings, including the New York City Police Department, the Long Island City Courthouse, and the Bank of America office in New York City. In 1971 twenty-two of its members were FBI fugitives.[14]

The Black Panther Party, formed in 1966 in a Negro slum in Oakland, California, has become a nationwide organization. In 1971 the Party had about 1000 members with thousands of sympathizers. Their official newspaper, *The Black Panther*, has a weekly circulation of about 100,000 copies. The Black Panthers have waged battles with police and made one attack upon the California State Capitol. They have demanded exemption of blacks from military service and amnesty for those now in prison. A serious rift developed in the Party in 1971 between Supreme Commander Huey P. Newton and Minister of Information Eldridge Cleaver, and Newton expelled Cleaver and his staff from the Party. In early 1972 Newton announced that the Black Panthers had rejected the "pick-up-the-gun-now" phi-

[12] "The 'New Left' in Action," *U.S. News & World Report*, May 19, 1969, p. 37. This article is used extensively for the data included in this paper on the New Left groups.
[13] Hoover, *op. cit.*, p. 70.
[14] *Ibid.*

losophy of Cleaver and would work through the system to bring about revolution.15 Included in his plan for working through the system were such tactics as the use of pickets to force merchants to contribute to the Party and voter registration drives in the Deep South.16

Student Afro-American Society, Black Student Union, and *Black Liberation Front* are three groups with similar aims and methodology. They attempt to recruit Negroes from large city slums for enrollment at predominantly white institutions. They attempt, sometimes by sit-ins and take-overs, to force compliance with demands for more black faculty, black studies courses, and in some instances separate facilities. All such groups combined probably numbered at their peak no more than 300,000 Negro students out of almost seven million students enrolled in U.S. colleges and universities. Frequently these groups have joined with SDS in making their demands known and felt.

Revolutionary Action Movement (RAM) was organized in 1963 in Detroit. It is composed of militant blacks dedicated to the overthrow of the capitalistic system in America and the installation of a socialistic system modeled after that of Red China. RAM operates under tight secrecy, but members have been charged with long-range plans to assassinate high officials and to murder policemen. The organization follows the teaching of Robert F. Williams. Some of his writings tell how to engage in sabotage by plugging sewer lines, starting fires, and paralyzing traffic.

The Youth International Party (YIP) grew from an idea conceived in 1967 in the apartment of Abbie Hoffman. The members, frequently known as "Yippies," express their aim as being that of destroying "the Man," their term for the present government. This group has little organization and is really more a philosophy of protest and ridicule than a movement of action. This is the group that joined with SDS in crippling the Democratic National Convention in Chicago. The major activ-

15 James O. Clifford, "Panthers Now Working in System, Newton Says," *The Nashville Tennessean,* January 31, 1972, p. 1.
16 *Ibid.*

ity of the group is to operate an underground press which has published about two hundred anti-establishment publications, many of them obscene.

The Progressive Labor Party was formed in 1962 by a group of young leftists who were expelled from the Communist Party USA because of their stand favoring Red China. The group, which has over three hundred members plus numerous sympathizers, seeks to form an alliance between students and workers and has been related to the Black Liberation Commission, headed by William Epton. The Progressive Labor Party is committed to a ceaseless struggle against the ruling class and it follows the doctrines of Mao Tse-tung in seeking to overthrow the present American form of government.

The Young Socialist Alliance, a Marxist organization founded in 1960, aggressively seeks to recruit college and high school students as members. It claimed a membership of about two thousand at the end of the 1969 school year. Its goal is the destruction of capitalism and imperialism.

What shall be said of all these groups? Gene Bradley has suggested that the uniformity of action, the similarity of objectives from campus to campus, the rapport among chapters, and the ability to mount massive protests such as the march on the Pentagon all point to some sort of organized international conspiracy directed from a central headquarters.[17] This idea has also been expressed by others, especially Governor Ronald Reagan of California. Bradley goes on to say that no one can prove that the New Left is connected with the Communist Party in Moscow, Peking, or Havana. All indications suggest that the New Left does not have a single international sponsor. United States intelligence officials have said as much, although they indicate that some financial support may be given to the professional student agitators. This money, investigators say, is "riding piggy-back on a tiger already on the loose."[18]

[17] "Goals of the 'New Left'—Down with Everything," *U.S. News & World Report*, January 20, 1969.
[18] *Newsweek*, March 10, 1969, p. 66.

Many observers, far from seeing all the groups working together, believe one of the weaknesses of the movement is that there are so many groups that are not sufficiently coordinated. A distinct difference can be seen between many of the black movements and the rest of the New Left. For the most part, the blacks still want a bigger piece of the American pie, while the New Left as a whole wants to destroy the pie. If the movement ever became one in purpose and methodology, it would have considerably more strength than it has today. Fragmented though it is, it has left its mark on American society and will continue to do so.[19]

The Radical Right

Extremism on the right in American society has been in existence for a much longer period of time, is more highly organized, and is much better financed than that on the left. It has made its influence felt upon politics, as well as American religion, for many years. Let us look at some of the more significant groups that are active in America today, although of necessity the treatment must be brief.

The *John Birch Society* was named after a Baptist missionary murdered by Chinese Communists shortly after Japan capitulated in 1945. John Birch had nothing to do with the organization and his name was selected only to lend weight to the war on Communism. The Society grew out of a founding conference held in December, 1958, in Indianapolis. The founder, Robert Welch, invited eleven men to the conference, where he delivered an address that consumed a major part of two days. What he said forms what has become known as *The Blue Book*, the bible and handbook of the John Birch Society. Welch called for "disciplined pullers at the oars, and not passengers in the boat." The John Birch Society would be a "monolithic body" operating

---

[19] For an analysis of the various types of students who compose some of these campus groups, see Gordon Blackwell and L. D. Johnson, "The Campus Crisis: The Generation Gap," *Review and Expositor*, Supplement 1969.

under completely authoritative control at all levels. The power of decision would belong to Welch. There would be an advisory council but it would advise only. Any person guilty of disloyalty would be purged, and each member agreed in his signed membership document that his membership could be rescinded "without reason being stated" by the "duly appointed officer of the Society."

The first chapter of the Society was established in January, 1959. Two years later Welch announced that chapters of the John Birch Society were in existence in thirty-four states and the District of Columbia, with a hundred chapters in California alone. The Society has continued to grow through the years and no one knows how large it is now.

There are four significant publications of the Society. In *The Blue Book*, mentioned above, Welch says, "We are fighting communists—nobody else." The list of persons to fight reveals that Welch has a strange criterion for identifying communists. They are liberals, the "hazy characters" whom Welch cannot trust. Many prominent political persons have been so listed, including Dwight Eisenhower and Allen Dulles. It was in *The Politician*, a publication that the John Birch Society did not officially sponsor but used extensively, that Welch made his charges concerning Eisenhower. The Society has never adopted the writing as one of its documents, but it is used as if it were official. The Society publishes a monthly *Bulletin;* and a journal, *American Opinion*, is edited by Welch. It is in the last publication that the question technique is used to smear outstanding citizens. Many articles are deliberately designed to smear persons Welch would like to destroy. He describes his technique in *The Blue Book*, on page 74, where he explains that one can write an article consisting entirely of questions to a man, questions which would be "devastating in implications." Welch goes on to say, "The question technique, when skillfully used in this way, is mean and dirty. But the Communists we are after are meaner and dirtier, and too slippery for you to get your finger on them in the ordinary way . . . ." These kinds of writings receive wide circulation and are frequently placed in doctors' and dentists' offices, barber shops, and reading rooms.

The John Birch Society operates on a utilitarian ethic. In the 1960 presidential campaign, Mr. Nixon said of the John Birch Society, "One of the most indelible lessons of American history is that those who adopt the doctrine that the end justifies the means inevitably find the means become the end." The John Birch Society has confused means and ends and has used the smear technique of guilt by association in such a way as to threaten the individual freedom and reputation of many loyal Americans.

The Dan Smoot Report. Dan Smoot was born in Missouri in 1913, grew up in Texas, received his education at Southern Methodist University and Harvard, served in the military, and then was employed by the FBI. In 1951 he began to produce a radio program, "Facts Forum," sponsored by H. L. Hunt in Dallas until 1955. The program proposed to state facts regarding issues and persons, but it inevitably slanted the facts to tilt opinion toward one side. Smoot said of the programs that he had received "well over 100,000 letters, most of them from people who liked the nationalist, pro-American, anti-communist, anti-socialist, anti-big-government side of the broadcast." It is no surprise that the public preferred this side of the broadcast because his programs were always slanted toward that side and he himself preferred that side. In 1955 he started his own "free enterprise" publication to give only one side. At first the new program was called *Dan Smoot Speaks*, but eight months later the name was changed to *The Dan Smoot Report*. The printed document has a tendency to be anti-communist, anti-civil rights, and anti-liquor. He slants his reports and fills them with partial truths in an obvious effort to persuade his readers to believe what he wants them to believe. His report is among the publications that the John Birch Society puts in doctors' offices and reading rooms.

Carl McIntire was born in Michigan in 1906, was reared in Oklahoma, and received his education in Missouri and at Princeton Seminary before receiving a degree at Westminster Seminary in 1931. After being dismissed from his denomination in 1936 he formed a splinter church of his own.

McIntire, says one observer, has demonstrated "an inability to work comfortably, and as an equal among equals, in any group where divergent views are represented" and has a "tendency to adopt toward target persons and groups the attitude of the avenger: the avenger whose arm is the elect instrument for striking down those who have departed from the truth."[20] McIntire apparently believes that he is the holder of the truth and that those who differ from him must be attacked. He cannot tolerate any dissent from his views. He wages especially strong attacks on the National Council of Churches.

Myers G. Lowman and the Circuit Riders. This group was formed in 1951 by thirty-three Methodist laymen who opposed socialism and communism in the Methodist Church. The Methodist Church took their word seriously and acted upon their report in 1952, and most of the group's demands were met. Nevertheless the Circuit Riders did not disband. Lowman retained whatever members he could and has since used the Circuit Riders for his own purpose, loosely organized but structured enough to claim tax exemption. As Executive Secretary of the Circuit Riders, Lowman has compiled multiple lists of suspected communists, especially clergymen. In addition, he lectures on communism and serves as consultant to school systems to identify com-

[20] Harry and Bonaro Overstreet, *The Strange Tactics of Extremism* (New York: Norton, 1964), pp. 148-149. This book is one of the finest dealing with the topic of extremism and is used here to aid in the description of the various groups mentioned. Other books that the author found useful include:

David M. Chalmers, *Hooded Americanism* (Garden City: Doubleday, 1965).

Brooks R. Walker, *The Christian Fright Peddlers* (Garden City: Doubleday, 1964).

Donald Janson and Bernard Eismann, *The Far Right* (New York: McGraw-Hill, 1963).

William Pierce Randall, *The Ku Klux Klan* (New York: Chilton Books, 1965).

munists, pro-communists, and leftists in schools and to evaluate school textbooks. Lowman is used frequently by Billy James Hargis as a speaker for his Christian Crusade programs. The John Birch Society calls on him to supply names of suspected communists to Welch.

Lowman's compilation of the names of suspect ministers includes 2,109 Methodists, 614 Presbyterians, 1,411 Protestant Episcopalians, 660 Baptists, 450 rabbis, 42 percent of all Unitarians, 30 of 95 persons who worked on the Revised Standard Version of the Bible, and 658 persons connected with the National Council of Churches. The Methodist Church undertook to research this matter and found that only 18 of the 2,109 Methodist clergymen named by Lowman had any serious and sustained connections with communism or with communist organizations. Again it becomes evident that Lowman has a peculiar definition for communism and is very quick to put people into that camp.

Edgar C. Bundy and the Church League of America. Bundy was born in Connecticut in 1915, received his schooling in Florida and at Wheaton College, and then served in the Air Force. While in the Air Force he was ordained in 1932 as a Southern Baptist minister in Louisiana. Following his military service, Bundy never served as a pastor but became editor of the *Daily Journal* in Wheaton, Illinois. Later he became Executive Secretary of the Church League of America; while this league dates from 1937, its policies today are those made by Bundy. He edits *News and Views*, a monthly. His writings claim to be based on research, but often his limited documentation does not justify branding an individual as a communist or as having communistic leanings. At times he resorts to the smear technique and the guilt-by-association approach, as is evident in his book, *Collectivism in the Churches*, published in 1958.

Billy James Hargis and the Christian Crusade. Hargis was born in Texas in 1925 and educated in Arkansas. Ordained at the age of 18, he served as pastor of churches in Oklahoma and Missouri and in 1945 brought the Christian Crusade into existence, calling it "a force for God and against communism." He moved the Crusade's headquarters to Tulsa and in 1954 put the promotional aspect into professional hands. The Crusade has grown rapidly since then: it now has radio and television broadcasts and publishes the monthly *Christian Crusade* and the *Weekly Crusader*. The Christian Crusade sponsors rallies and conferences, conducts a summer youth school in Colorado, sponsors youth chapters called "Torchbearers," and provides a platform for speakers. Hargis has made use of other extremists, and in turn they have used him and his materials.

His anticommunism is not based on good information, and "communism" in his view seems to include all religious, social, political, and economic attitudes and policies of which he disapproves. His messages and writings frequently contain undocumented assertions presented as facts. For example, he contends that he knows of textbooks that have been "revised and rewritten" under communist orders. But he refuses to reveal any of his evidence, if indeed he has any.

The Ku Klux Klan. The Klan was officially organized on December 24, 1865, with the overt purpose of restoring white supremacy to the South by intimidating the freed Negro slaves and their white supporters. It became sufficiently strong to accomplish its purposes through fear and intimidation. A second major period of activity for the Klan was during and after World War One, when it is reported to have secured six million members. In addition to its racial emphasis, the Klan at this time continued to be strongly against Jews, Catholics, and the foreign-born. Not only did it support white supremacy, but it had a strongly moral authoritarianism. The Klan frequently took action against persons engaging in immoral activities.

The Klan came into prominence in some southern states again in the 1960's and gained several thousand members before state governments took action to block it. The Klan has fallen into disrepute in recent years, largely as a result of official legal action taken against it. Several of its members have been imprisoned and others have been cited for contempt of Congress.

Several books published recently recount the first

hundred years of the Klan's existence. All of them have warned that the Klan must not be taken lightly even today, difficult though it is for many of us to understand how an organization can gain members in America when it proposes and practices a gospel of hate, fear, and lawlessness.

It is generally recognized that there are innumerable radical right-wing organizations in the nation. Obviously no one researcher can identify all of these. Some of those usually listed in research documents are the National Socialist White People's Party (formerly the American Nazi Party), the Minutemen, the Manion Forum, the National Economic Council, and Fred Schwarz's Christian Anti-Communist Crusade.[21] While the first two may include only a few hundred emotionally disturbed persons, the others are much better financed and reach millions of Americans through their propaganda and radio and television programs.

The organizations mentioned in this chapter are guilty of turning their wrath toward persons who differ with their extreme views and of inciting a kind of hatred and fear that should not be encouraged. This is the reason that we must be concerned about extremism, whether it be on the left or the right. Christians must be cautious in their treatment of extremist groups, lest they also become guilty of extremism. Thoughtful people need to try to discover the facts, use them in a responsible manner, and steadfastly refuse to be taken in by the extremists, whose philosophy and methodology can only degrade the quality of life in America.

---

[21] Robert A. Rosenstone, *Protest from the Right* (Beverly Hills: Glencoe Press, 1968).

4

Sources of Extremism

C. Arthur Insko

The contemporary American scene is marked by a growing fragmentation of the social fabric which holds the nation together. While the majority of citizens are committed to a national purpose amid the complexities and problems of a revolutionary age, a growing minority are disillusioned with the values of the society.

The decade of the sixties was a time of national soul-searching in the midst of the most searing criticism at home and abroad. One consequence of the social upheavals is a growing awareness of racism, violence, and anxiety within America at a time of global power and responsibility. Extremist groups have dramatized the deep cleavages with increasing vigor and militancy.

In this situation Peter Berger has warned of the twin dangers of tyranny from the right and chaos from the left. He voices a legitimate fear that the power of government will be used in a "lawless, oppressive or inhuman" way.[1] On the other hand, he thinks the continuing destructive protests can bring a political situation "in which orderly government disintegrates and

---

[1] Peter Berger, "Between Tyranny and Chaos," *Christian Century*, October 30, 1968, p. 1365.

C. Arthur Insko is Professor of Christian Ethics, Golden Gate Baptist Theological Seminary, Mill Valley, California.

Hobbesian forms of brute violence replace what we commonly call civilization."[2]

Whether or not they agree with this rather alarmist view of the present situation, all sober-minded citizens are deeply troubled by the threats to freedom and civil order. Such concern does not deny the right of dissent but is motivated by recognition that the dangers of each new confrontation by the militants will also encourage the forces of reaction.

In a democratic society some balance must be maintained between the freedom to demand "redress of grievance" and the necessity for orderly and peaceful change. But extremist movements differ markedly from loyal opposition or responsible dissent. With ideologies based on a distorted view of reality, extremists absolutize a given historical situation and pursue their illusions with apocalyptic fervor. Speaking of the "paranoid style" of the radical right, Richard Hofstadter says, the extremist "traffics in the birth and death of whole worlds, whole political systems, whole systems of human value."[3] Such illusions pose a severe threat to the sanity of society.

Extremism finds expression in movements that are poles apart in ideology. Yet their thought and action have a common origin. Berger insists that the left and the right are intimately related and mutually supportive. For this reason he contends that "the foremost moral imperative of our situation is to resist and combat both of them simultaneously."[4]

We must be careful that in combating extremism we do not become extremist. The extremist's tendency to oversimplify complex issues is contagious. Moreover, extremism often feeds on problems that do need the serious attention of responsible groups in society. Its legitimate fears and just grievances must be dealt with.

While extremism may be fundamentally a psychic phenomenon, its elements arise from the cultural con-

[2] *Ibid.*

[3] Richard Hofstadter, "The Paranoid Style in American Politics," *Harper's,* November, 1964, p. 82.

[4] Berger, *op. cit.,* p. 1365.

text in which it appears. It is the purpose of this paper to identify the principal sources of extremism in American life.

A National Inheritance

There is in the American ethos a certain proneness to extremism and violence. The frontier spirit and the six-shooter are part of our tradition. As a nation we were born in revolution. The elite New Left attempts to find the intellectual roots of radicalism in the American tradition of freedom beginning with the Declaration of Independence. Although this is a distortion of our history, it is true that manifestations of radicalism or extremism today are in part a legacy of our political and social experience.

For one thing, the rough-and-tumble style of American politics generates all kinds of exaggerations. Wild charges and extravagant claims have long been used for vote-getting. Sociologist Seymour Lipset says, "The lack of an aristocratic tradition in American politics helped to prevent the emergence of a moderate rhetoric in political life."[5]

Bring to this unrestrained process the animosities, frustrations, and fantasies of what Hofstadter calls the "paranoid style" of mind, and restraint and rationality give way to sheer hatemongering. Politics then becomes, according to Hofstadter, "an arena for angry minds.... a recurrent phenomenon in our public life which has frequently been linked with movements of suspicious discontent."[6]

In the past a number of extremist groups and persons have risen to prominence and occasionally to some power. The Know-Nothing Party, for example, a movement protesting immigration and favoring the exclusion of the foreign-born from full citizenship, received 25

---

[5] Seymour Lipset, "The Sources of the Radical Right," in *The Radical Right*, ed. Daniel Bell (New York: Doubleday, 1963), p. 266.

[6] Hofstadter, *op. cit.*, p. 77.

percent of the popular vote in the election of 1856. In the early decades of this century the Ku Klux Klan was a decisive political influence in some areas, particularly in the South. This is not to infer that all the people influenced by these groups were mentally unbalanced. Hofstadter thinks the phenomenon is significant because of "the use of paranoid modes of expression by more or less normal people."[7]

One recurring phenomenon has been the illusion that certain groups or powers, domestic or foreign, are conspiring to destroy our basic rights. Hofstadter regards this as the classic illustration of paranoia in our body politic. He shows how it has been a prime motivation for extremist groups from the anti-Masonic and anti-Catholic movements in our earlier history to those on both sides of the race issue today, ardent segregationists as well as black militants.[8]

The right-wing John Birch Society is a well-known contemporary movement playing on fears of communist subversion. Its fundamental tenet is that for a generation communists have been infiltrating the government and community life and are secretly engineering an ultimate take-over. The Society's founder, Robert Welch, has said, "Not only our federal government but our state governments are to a disturbing extent captives of the Communists."[9] The absurdity of this claim was revealed when John Foster Dulles and President Eisenhower were named as members of this communist conspiracy. Mark Sherwin has pointed to the tragedy of the extreme right: "With exaggerated fears and a lamentable lack of confidence in the Government, these people have organized to fight Communism on their own wild and irresponsible level, and have themselves been used as dupes to press for ideas that have nothing to do with the battle against Communism."[10]

[7] *Ibid.*

[8] *Ibid.*, p. 78.

[9] Robert Welch, *The New Americanism* (Boston: Western Islands, 1966), p. 58.

[10] Mark Sherwin, *The Extremists* (New York: St. Martin's Press, 1963), pp. 12-13.

The tensions of the Cold War have spawned an even more radical group known as the Minutemen. With a cache of arms and plans ready for execution, these vigilantes are eager to defend our freedom in what they see as the coming battle with communism in America. Mark Sherwin calls this self-styled guerrilla force "the psychotic, serio-comic exaggeration of the wildest dreams of the Far Right."[11]

Why this obsession with threats, real or imagined, to the American people? It comes in part from social pressures for conformity to our political and cultural values. Lipset holds that Americanism is a "compulsive ideology," stemming from our revolutionary tradition and the immigrant character of our society. Belief in the superiority of the American political system and the status attained by becoming an American produce a deep concern for ideological conformity. He concludes, "It is this emphasis on ideological conformity to presumably common political values that legitimatizes the hunt for 'un-Americans' in our midst."[12]

Commitment to an American creed has often been accompanied by a pervasive intolerance, particularly toward minority groups. The source of intolerance may lie in unconscious arrogance, resulting from the feelings of superiority mentioned earlier. Lipset believes it is an inheritance of Protestant puritanical morality that insists on an absolute difference between right and wrong. He sees "this propensity . . . most evident, and perhaps most disastrous in the area of foreign policy where allies and enemies cannot be gray, but must be black or white."[13]

In any case, our record of intolerance has been a shameful one. Throughout our history many racial and ethnic groups have been denied basic rights because of their different racial or cultural backgrounds and beliefs. To this day some citizens and groups would deny a person the right to run for the presidency because of his

[11] *Ibid.*, p. 156.
[12] Lipset, *op. cit.*, p. 268.
[13] *Ibid.*, p. 265.

religious beliefs. And the persistence of anti-Semitism is evidence of a continuing intolerance. "It seems evident," Lipset concludes, "that at all times many Americans have been in favor of denying basic civil liberties to beliefs that they have found abhorrent."[14] In the extremist superpatriot this is often expressed as a righteous wrath against foreign or subversive influences alien to the white, Anglo-Saxon, Protestant majority.

Protestant Nativism and Modern Individualism

Closely allied with this superpatriotism is a Protestant nativism which insists that America has always been a Christian nation and that every effort must be made to guard or restore this heritage. The founding fathers are romanticized, and a sentimentalized image of the early days becomes the standard for all succeeding ages. It is the backward look that characterizes all reactionary thinking. To be sure, we are the inheritors of a great tradition. But its genius is not preserved by an idolatrous Americanism.

Basically, this nativist nationalism is concerned with preserving the remnants of the Protestant establishment. It is unwilling or unable to accept pluralism in American society and strongly opposed to any changes that threaten the old foundations of Protestant supremacy. Thus the efforts to preserve Bible-reading in the public schools have become a crusade to "keep America Christian." Much anti-Catholicism, anti-Semitism, anti-refugee sentiment, racism, and nativism of ultraconservative Protestant groups, according to Franklin Littell, "derives its support from islands of defensive culture-religion which resent being passed by in the flow of national history."[15]

Of all the elements in our national heritage that contribute to extremism, none is more significant than the modern individualistic view of man. It is basic in the

[14] *Ibid.*, p. 368.
[15] Franklin Littell, *From State Church to Pluralism* (New York: Doubleday, 1962), p. 59.

ideology of extremists from both the left and the right today.

Right-wing extremism is a fusing of the nineteenth-century doctrine of rugged individualism with ultraconservative Protestant fundamentalism. In a sense these are contradictory views of the nature and destiny of man. Eighteenth- and nineteenth-century individualism was the flowering of the Renaissance doctrine of man, rooted in classical humanist thought. It breathed the modern spirit of freedom and autonomy for man. But the fundamentalist doctrine of the total depravity of man, set in a strong eschatological framework, denounces such a this-worldly view and looks for an apocalyptic end to the proud pretensions of man as God comes in wrath to judge the world.

Despite these inconsistencies, the contemporary fundamentalist is the staunchest defender of the rights and freedoms of the individual. Here is a classic example of the marriage of religion with the spirit of the age. The tension between faith and culture has been dissolved. Christianity is interpreted in largely individualistic terms. The biblical view of man as a person in community is ignored and the social dimension of the gospel is denied. Religion becomes a lonely affair between the individual and his God. Moreover, the individual is the primary agent in the salvation experience. Thus individualistic, man-centered religion is born. The prophetic dimension of the biblical faith is lost in a surrender to cultural norms and values.

As a culture religion, fundamentalist extremism has adopted in toto the economic individualism of the nineteenth century. It sings the glories of capitalism. Even the Darwinian emphasis on "struggle for existence" and "survival of the fittest" is taken up by the economic conservative, according to Hofstadter, in the form of the idea that "Nature would provide that the best competitors in a competitive situation would win, and that this process would lead to a continuing improvement."[16]

[16] Richard Hofstadter, *Social Darwinism in American Thought* (Boston: Beacon Press, 1944), p. 6.

In this context social concern and community action become suspect. Government welfare programs are attacked as "creeping socialism," a threat to our cherished American way of life. And so masses of people in need are sacrificed on the altar of a reactionary ideology which denies the Christian imperative to love one's neighbor.

We find modern individualism in leftist extremism as well. Communism seeks the collectivization of society in the interest of the common man. But it destroys genuine community among men by its commitment to class warfare. Comradeship is based on the appeal to selfish interest, a kind of individualism, and a common hatred for the enemies of the working classes. In the end it sacrifices the individual to the faceless mass and makes personal identity of no consequence.

Communism is not the wave of the future. It is a nineteenth-century ideology that is increasingly anachronistic in the twentieth century. Maintained by subversion and the power of the ruling cliques, communism faces growing criticism from the younger generation in communist as well as non-communist countries. As John Cogley points out, the new idea of politics emerging in the youth revolution throughout the world is based on "a new perception not of political reality but of human reality."[17]

This youth movement includes a strain of nineteenth-century existentialism, which protested the threat to the individual posed by the impersonal forces of industrial society. The economic man of that time was a distortion of full humanity. Likewise, political man in the twentieth century, the youth believe, is less than a whole person, his freedom and authentic existence taken away by tyrannical forces. Thus the continuing legacy of modern individualism is a part of the powerful influence of existentialist thought today.

---

[17] John Cogley, "Political Reality and Human Reality," *Worldview*, vol. XI, no. 1 (January, 1968), p. 12.

A New Radicalism

The concern for authentic selfhood is a positive emphasis in the youth revolution. But we also find negative elements in the radicalism expressed by contemporary militant and student protests. The radicals are explicit in their rejection of the values and institutions of contemporary society. They have no faith in the processes of evolutionary change. The "Establishment" must be destroyed.

To be sure, this is the view of a small minority, but on many campuses it has gained considerable support. So far it appears that militant black leaders have received no more than token support from the Negro masses.

Undoubtedly there are anarchists among the hard-core militants on campus and in the Black Power groups. But their number is small. But nihilism seems to influence a significant number of the protesters. Theologian Robert Fitch found at the heart of the Berkeley student revolt a "value vacuum," a great "yawning void" resulting from the skepticism, relativism, impressionism, existentialism, "which have cast out all structures, patterns, imperatives, laws, principles, standards, leaving only chaos and dark night to rule over the ruin."[18] Revolt for some is becoming a way of life, and some radicals seek a continuing chaos. Violence is regarded as a utopia.

Moreover, acts of terror are justified on the pretext that they are necessary to dramatize the evils of the system. This reflects the Marxist idea that what is right is that which advances the revolution.

Marxism is ideologically linked with the New Left revolution. Some militants are clearly Maoist, but no definite link with communist or foreign subversive elements has been established. While there are marked similarities in the youth revolution from country to

[18] Robert E. Fitch, "Extremism in the Defense of . . . ," in *The Berkeley Student Revolt*, ed. Lipset and Wolin (New York: Doubleday, 1965), p. 401.

country, domestic issues and conditions usually spark rebellion.

In discussing the ecology of student discontent, Lloyd Averill has said, "The campus culture tends to reinforce the sense of futility that the students bring with them from the larger culture."[19] Why this sense of futility? What conditions in the larger culture produce the angry discontent of extremists, right and left?

Revolutionary Change

Much extremism has its source in the monumental changes taking place in society. Revolutionary change is a fundamental fact of life today. In a scientific and technological revolution, American society is adopting new modes of life and thought. And the pace of change is so rapid that adjustments are nearly impossible for some segments of society. It is not surprising that extremist behavior is one result.

According to Talcott Parsons, it is well established in the social sciences "that neither individuals nor societies can undergo major structural changes without the likelihood of producing a considerable element of irrational behavior."[20] Under the stresses of change, both one's values and one's comprehension of the facts of a situation will be greatly distorted. "These distorted beliefs and promptings to irrational action will also tend to be heavily weighted with emotion."[21]

Emotional responses to change will manifest both aggressive and regressive tendencies, according to Parsons. The aggressive response seeks to eliminate the threat or supposed source of the danger. On the other hand, the regressive tendency functions "to wish away the disturbing situation and establish a situation in phantasy where everything will be all right."[22] Such

[19] Lloyd Averill, "The Ecology of Discontent," *Christian Century*, June 18, 1969, p. 835.

[20] Talcott Parsons, "Social Strains in America," in *The Radical Right*, ed. Daniel Bell (New York: Doubleday, 1963), p. 182.

[21] *Ibid.*

[22] *Ibid.*

reactions are not serious in the normal process of change, but they become dangerous when heightened by the fears and frustrations of social turmoil, war, and the threat of atomic destruction.

Today Americans are experiencing severe strains, both internal and external. The race problem at home and the war in Southeast Asia are agonizing burdens. The nation is frustrated. For the first time we face the limitations of our awesome power. Many problems seem insoluble. The future is frightfully complex and dangerous. As Robert Lee says, "Finding it difficult to live in such a world, we seek scapegoats for our frustrations and hostilities."[23]

Growing Alienation

Another source of extremism today is the growing sense of alienation arising from our mass culture. Youth are revolting against the impersonal, confining, manipulative structures of what they regard as an evil society. Therefore they demand a radical restructuring of the whole social order. Among youthful idealists this can become an obsession. Some of the more militant groups think the justice of their cause places them outside the law and gives them the freedom to pillage and destroy.

There are constructive as well as destructive aspects of this rejection of the patterns of the culture. John Cogley says the resistance to political, social, corporate, ecclesiastic, military, and educational structures that have become self-perpetuating or self-seeking "is basically sound, though it has led to some absurd posturing, to self-deception, mindless rebellion and a library of thoughtless slogans passing for thought."[24] This seems a rather indulgent assessment in the face of the violence and non-negotiable demands of some militants. But Cogley maintains that the beginnings of every lasting movement in history have had excesses and that the excesses

---

[23] Robert Lee, "Social Sources of the Radical Right," *Christian Century*, May 9, 1962, pp. 595-596.

[24] John Cogley, *op. cit.*, p. 13.

of the youth revolution are incidental to its significance for the years ahead.25

The reactions to the technological revolution are profound. Intelligent, affluent youth are sensing the fallacies of a messianic scientism and the emptiness in the triumph of technological man. They reject the impersonal efficiency of a computerized society because it leads to mass conformity and threatens self-identity and the quality of human relationships. Hence their opposition to institutions which seek to use persons as means in achieving organizational ends. The youthful protesters insist on a voice in the making of decisions that vitally affect their lives.

Certainly this protest needs serious consideration. In a theological perspective, perhaps we can see a judgment on our society in the crisis of meaning and values. While the anarchist elements are dangerous and have to be controlled, there are underlying concerns in the youth protests that can contribute to the improvement of our culture. A conformist, success-oriented, acquisitive society needs to pay more attention to the more important human values which are at the heart of American ideals. Youth are right to rebel against their elders' hypocritical commitment to values which they deny in practice. The protesters' condemnation of this basic dishonesty is a healthy development.

Leftist youth are not alone in their frustration and estrangement. The same mass society is also the source of alienation on the right. The rising pay scale has kept the blue-collar worker docile, but he too feels a deep estrangement from the impersonal organizations in which he is a number rather than a person. Gabriel Fackre maintains that laboring-class alienation is "as severe, disorienting, and thingifying [sic] as that felt by the black, the young and the poor."26 The two basic ingredients are loss of identity and lack of a voice in controlling the modern industrial process. Like other

---

25 *Ibid.*

26 Gabriel Fackre, "The Blue Collar White and the Far Right," *Christian Century*, May 7, 1969, p. 645.

alienated groups in society, says Fackre, "the blue collar workers have been afflicted with a sense of powerlessness. And as they are powerless, they are loveless."[27]

Persons who are dehumanized by the mass culture are easy marks for those leaders skilled in making political capital of social discontent. For example, many blue-collar workers in the 1968 election supported the rightist American Independence Party of George Wallace, because they were given a voice and a cause with which they could identify. Simplistic solutions were offered for complex modern problems, and victory over the big impersonal foe was promised. This got a wide response from the ranks of labor.

Class and Race Conflicts

A principal source of extremist behavior is the threat of growing class and race conflicts. These problems in the United States reflect the rising power of the enslaved peoples of the world. The rightist defenders of the status quo have cause to fear this revolution. The non-white peoples and the have-nots of the world are determined to have their freedom and to share in the benefits of the scientific and technological revolution. Everywhere the welfare society is growing nearer.

In America, the social welfare conflict has a history of more than a generation. Since the New Deal of the 1930's there has been a strong rightist reaction to welfare programs for the dispossessed. Many right-wing extremists still see Franklin D. Roosevelt as the arch-enemy of the American system of free enterprise. According to them he first brought on the evils of the welfare state.

Professor Lipset has described two political forces operating under varying historical conditions which help explain political extremism in the United States. He calls these forces "status politics" and "class politics." The latter is defined as "political division based on discord between the traditional left and the right, i.e.,

[27] *Ibid.*, p. 647.

those favoring the redistribution of income and those favoring the preservation of the status-quo."[28] Status politics refers to "political movements whose appeal is to the not uncommon resentments of individuals and groups who desire to maintain or improve their social status."[29]

Status-conscious groups are vocal in times of growing affluence when large numbers of people have moved up the economic scale. They have risen to a new status, and they fear the loss of some of their gains to minorities lower on the scale. The present strength of the radical right among blue-collar workers is a striking illustration of status politics. Individuals who were formerly a part of the depressed masses, in ideological affinity with minority groups, now fear the growing power and influence of the same groups in the human rights struggle. In this struggle, as Gabriel Fackre points out, the blue-collar workers have been "those frontiers of white society that were most directly affected by the structural changes in the patterns of housing, education, and jobs."[30]

Status politics also affects older groups in society who are fearful of losing the privileges they hold in the upheavals of rapid social change. Robert Lee refers to these as the group that is "descending" while the blue-collar workers are "ascending" the status ladder. In either case, says Lipset, "Political movements which have successfully appealed to status resentments have been irrational in character and have sought scapegoats which conveniently symbolize the status threat."[31] Among popular scapegoats today are the courts, the press, and the "bureaucrats in Washington." Traditionally they have most often been ethnic and religious minorities.

These minorities used as scapegoats are frequently the dispossessed who are seeking the rights and privileges

[28] Lipset, *op. cit.*, p. 260.
[29] *Ibid.*
[30] Fackre, *op. cit.*, p. 646.
[31] Lipset, *op. cit.*, pp. 260-261.

SOURCES OF EXTREMISM

enjoyed by the majority. This is the struggle of the Negro minority now. Frustration, born of deprivation in the midst of widespread freedom and wealth, has produced the extremist black militants. And white opposition to legitimate demands will create many more. That they absolutize the evils of the white power structure is at least understandable. They have lost patience with the civil rights movement and are demanding support for the building of a separate black power base.

Hofstadter sees the confrontation of opposed interests or irreconcilable differences as the principal source of the paranoid tendency in all extremism. Moreover, the situation is always made worse when one group is kept out of the political process. "Having no access to political bargaining or the making of decisions, they find their original conception that the world of power is sinister and malicious, fully confirmed."[32]

At the same time, a representative of the power structure such as the white supremacist absolutizes the racial and social differences between whites and blacks to justify his segregationist stance. As the legal barriers between the races have come down, the frustrations of the segregationist have been intensified. He knows that the changes are irresistible in the long run. However, he obstructs the process wherever he can in the hope of delaying the inevitable. Meanwhile he nurses his hatred, at a frightful cost to himself and his children. Since no enduring social order can be built on such bitterness, his extremism, like that of the black militant, becomes both a personal and a social tragedy. And so the evil is compounded.

Financial Support

As has been noted, extremism in a variety of expressions has been a feature of American life since early days. But the radical right groups have seen significant growth in the period since World War Two. The frustra-

---

[32] Richard Hofstadter, "The Paranoid Style in American Politics," p. 86.

tions of the cold war and the turmoil of rapid social change have generated new fears.

The widespread affluence of the postwar period is another contributing factor. As Lipset pointed out, anxieties over status are more acute in prosperity. Fear of losing newly acquired wealth can lead men into rightist movements promising protection, whose leaders capitalize on these fears to gain financial support. And so a state of affluence is doubly advantageous to the promoters of the radical right.

There are at present a number of rightist organizations that are generously staffed and financed. It is reported that Carl McIntire's operations gross three million dollars annually. Principal sources include the support of listeners to his widely disseminated radio programs, the newspaper *Christian Beacon*, and real estate ventures.

Other rightist movements have a variety of techniques for raising funds. Billy James Hargis underwrites his Christian Crusade through radio appeals, mass rallies, and publications. Fred Schwarz of the Christian Anti-Communism Crusade has depended heavily on his anti-communism schools and one-night rallies. The John Birch Society, with a yearly payroll of more than two million dollars, has a large dues-paying membership, extensive publication operations, bookstores, and radio programs. The Church League of America, directed by Edgar Bundy, has concentrated on publishing materials about organizations and individuals it considers subversive. It too has a dues-paying membership, publishes a magazine, sells books, and conducts seminars and radio broadcasts. Of course all these groups receive support through gifts large and small from loyal supporters.

Leading leftist and militant groups depend mainly on annual dues or assessments from members. They also receive support from personal solicitation and through mass rallies. The amount of support from international communism, if any, is not known.

In sum, these activities involve many thousands of people and millions of dollars in movements that stir up strife, create suspicion, and vilify the courts, some churches, and elected officials.

The average American is aware of the dangers in international communism and committed to the defense of democratic institutions. Continuing international tensions keep the public vigilant. Unfortunately, few are equally aware of the threat to basic liberties posed by the radical right groups. It needs to be stressed that freedom is in as much danger from the radical right as from the far left.

A Heavy Burden

To the problems of the real world, difficult enough for responsible persons, are added the burdens of those who have exaggerated fears and suspicions of their fellow men. Extremism is a double burden for society and for the individuals caught up in their illusions. As Hofstadter put it, "We are all sufferers from history, but the paranoid is a double sufferer . . . afflicted not only by the real world, . . . but by his fantasies as well."[33] The extremist's utopianism has no room for the paradoxical elements in all human existence.

To be human is to be subject to all the relativities of time and history. We cannot demand that the world conform to rigid systems and absolute categories. Absolutes are really very few. A moderate, flexible stance is the most healthful way to face the demands of a changing world.

It is not faith, but doubt and fear, that causes men to idolize the past. Whoever believes he is moving in God's world will face with hope even the shaking of the foundations that is going on today.

[33] *Ibid.*

5
Psychological Dimensions of Extremism

C. W. Scudder

The rapidity of change today staggers the imagination. James Reston of the *New York Times* has stated that "change is the biggest story in the world today."[1] Roger Shinn believes that people today are "quivering under the shock of change."[2] The almost inevitable result is confusion, anxiety, uncertainty, and fear. It is in such a time that we are considering extremism.

Serious consideration of the psychological dimensions of extremism requires definition of terms and a delineation of approach. Two basic psychoanalytic theories have been suggested: (1) the frustrated self, and (2) the authoritarian personality. Our subject might be dealt with under two main headings: (1) frustrated revolutionaries, and (2) authoritarian conservatives. But such a dichotomy is unnecessary if we view extremism as a phenomenon.

Some persons holding strong convictions feel threatened or intimidated by the use of the term "extremist." Strong convictions, however, do not necessarily consti-

---

[1] James Reston, "The Biggest Story in the World," *The New Republic*, May 4, 1963, p. 15.

[2] Roger Shinn, *Tangled World* (New York: Scribner's Sons, 1965), p. 9.

C. W. Scudder is Professor of Christian Ethics, Southwestern Baptist Theological Seminary, Fort Worth, Texas.

tute extremism. For example, the author of *Apostles of Discord* did not consider all fundamentalism extremism. In fact, he credited those whom he called "genuine fundamentalists" with having reached millions of people with "old-time religion" who might never have been reached by others. But he charged a "vociferous minority" with promoting conflict and confusion. He mentioned Charles E. Fuller as a "genuine fundamentalist" and Gerald L. K. Smith as one of the "vociferous minority."[3]

It is important that we differentiate between the loyal, concerned critic and the irresponsible, revolutionary agitator. Prophets have served as the most creative force within the Christian movement, and there have always been those who have sought to discredit and silence prophetic leaders. The Christian Life Commission and those of us in the field of Christian ethics surely stand in the prophetic stream. We have often been threatened by those who would silence us. Do we deserve to be labeled as extremists? We shall need to answer that question in the light of the psychological dimensions of extremism.

The extremism with which we are concerned is more an attitude toward others than a set of beliefs, no matter with what degree of conviction they are held. Such extremism might be defined as an overresponse to a real or supposed threat coming from others. In any event, our concern is with extremism in relationships. Wayne Oates says that the extremist "interprets all relationships in terms of a power struggle. . . . Cooperation is foreign to him."[4] Extremism and cooperation are incompatible.

The psychologist is concerned with the phenomena of consciousness and behavior. The social psychologist is concerned about how we act in our relationships with others. Our concern in this study is clearly in the field of social psychology. We seek an understanding of ex-

[3] Ralph Lord Roy, *Apostles of Discord* (Boston: Beacon Press, 1953), p. x.

[4] Wayne E. Oates, *Pastoral Counseling in Social Problems* (Philadelphia: Westminster Press, 1966), p. 42.

tremism and of the social forces that affect or produce extremism. What are the characteristics of extremism and of extremists? Why are people extremists? What sociological phenomena contribute to extremist attitudes and motivate people to extremist activities?

Cynical Intolerance

First of all, extremism is characterized by a kind of cynical, deliberate intolerance. Because of their behavior, some campus militants have been compared to the "bully boys" of Hitler's Third Reich. Their extreme actions in disrupting university life and at times manhandling university personnel are viewed not as being incidental or spontaneous, but as springing "from a deliberately articulated philosophy of cynical intolerance—an intolerance that dialectically sports itself as tolerance."[5]

All extremism is pervaded by intolerance—indeed, it is the very essence of extremism. For extremists are unwilling to endure the views, opinions, and religious beliefs of others. They fence themselves into a world of their own, a world organized around their own "ism."

Intolerance expresses itself in many different ways. It cultivates suspicion and breeds distrust. It might be viewed as the mother of gossip—distorted, malicious gossip. Radical intolerance often explodes in expressions of hatred and acts of violence. In all cases it fosters division, in homes, churches, and political affairs.

Extremists seem almost to fear the views of others. They fear being corrupted. They do not want to be exposed. They close their minds to ideas different from their own. They profess to have an exclusive claim on truth. Their environment seems to them unfriendly, not to be trusted. The intolerance of closed-minded extremists is often reinforced by ethnic, national, or racial prejudice.[6] And it is well to remember that closed-

---

[5] *Christianity Today*, November 8, 1968, p. 32.

[6] Edgar Metzler, *Let's Talk About Extremism* (Scottdale, Pennsylvania: Herald Press, 1968), p. 10.

mindedness is characteristic of extremists holding widely different views. The rigidity and dogmatism of the Ku Klux Klan is very similar to that of black nationalism.

We all recognize that people can disagree without being disagreeable. It is possible for two people with strong convictions to hold different views and still respect each other. Not so with extremists. When intolerance enters the picture, people become disagreeable and disrespectful. Such is the nature of extremism.

Angry Frustration

Consideration of current social conditions causes many to become frustrated. Frustration may produce either resistance to change or a desire for change. Some are frustrated because they are unable to stop changes that are taking place. They seek to preserve the status quo. Their image of the way things ought to be is being shattered. They prefer no change at all, but if it must come, they want it to come about more slowly. Yet they seem to be unable even to decrease the rapidity of change. On the other hand, those people deprived of their rights by inequities and injustices, lacking the power to change things, have also become unbearably frustrated. Extremists in both groups are angry, and social unrest is the result. Speaking during a session of the Christian Life Commission Seminar in Chicago, Karl Olsson stated that "social unrest, however unwelcome and unpleasant, is a crude effort to restore the balance which injustice has destroyed."[7]

Those concerned about alleviating human need are frustrated by the priorities of churches and cities. Brooks Ramsey referred to announcements made by New York City churches concerning proposed building programs. "One church was to spend $350,000 to build a choir room and rooms for assistant pastors. Another was to spend $125,000 to increase the number of stops on its organ. Still another made known it plans to spend $850,000 to renovate the building, which renovation

---

[7] *Proceedings*, 1969 Christian Life Commission Seminar, p. 9.

was to consist mainly of cleaning the stones on the outside of the building.... During this same period, the state of New York announced that it was spending $60,000 to set up an experimental center for the rehabilitation of alcoholics." Ramsey posed the question: "In which of these activities do you suppose the Spirit of God was most interested?"[8] Concerned Christians can hardly fail to be frustrated by such priorities, and for some the frustration is intense.

Another kind of frustration has been pictured by Jesse Jackson. He referred to the fact that 1 percent of the population of a Southern state "receives more than $5,000,000 a year not to farm while more than fifty-three percent of its population receives less than one million dollars to survive." He stated that the United States Senator from another state "receives $13,000 a month not to farm" while "children on his plantation receive $9.00 a month to survive. Then," he said, "they escape to the North as refugees and riot out of frustration."[9] Frustration born out of such conditions is motivating an increasing number of people to extreme action.

A feeling of alienation is another fruit of frustration. The testimony of Jesse Jackson is well worth repeating: "When I was growing up in South Carolina," he said, "I wish I could have joined some of your churches, but I couldn't and that's part of the problem. You can escape up here, but there's a Southern Baptist church right up the street from my house on Anderson Street in Greenville; and if I got caught in there for anything other than being a janitor, I would probably get put in jail. That's the state of things," he concluded.[10] We had better hear these frustrated people who are still willing to talk with us. For the feeling of alienation may well change to anger.

J. Edgar Hoover recently spoke to a congressional committee concerning the New Left. He said: "The

[8] *Ibid.*, p. 62.
[9] *Ibid.*, p. 61.
[10] *Ibid.*, p. 57.

mood of this movement, which is best typified by its primary spokesman, the Students for a Democratic Society, is a mood of *disillusionment, pessimism* and *alienation.* At the center of the movement," he said, "is an almost passionate desire to destroy, to annihilate, to tear down."[11] The SDS provides one of the best demonstrations of angry frustration at its worst.

In their frustration, a growing number of young Americans have been turning to Marxism and the extreme left. Members of organizations such as the Black Panthers have openly expressed their commitment to Marxism. Karl Olsson evaluated the frustration of a less-revolutionary Marxist: "I understand the impatience of a Marxist friend who told me that she was willing to forget the beatitude of heavenly bread for the sake of a hundred million empty stomachs." He continued, "I honor her furious sense of justice. But despite its sin of forgetting the disaster of hunger, the church is compelled to proclaim that man does not live by bread alone."[12]

Certainly, the church is not to become a glorified soup kitchen; it has a broader mission than that. But we in the churches had better give serious attention to the impatience, alienation, and angry frustration of a growing number of people. And we had better listen well if we expect to get a hearing when we speak. Angry frustration is fast destroying the lines of communication between us and making true dialogue difficult if not impossible.

There is no justification for the destruction caused by angry frustration which we have witnessed in recent years. But neither is any American justified in ignoring the continuing inequities and injustices which produce angry frustration.

Paralyzing Fear

As frustration motivates most of the New Left, fear motivates most of the radical right. The authors of

[11] *U. S. News & World Report*, May 12, 1969, p. 34.
[12] *Proceedings*, p. 10.

Danger on the Right have stated that "there can be no doubt radical rightists are motivated by a hatred and fear of many twentieth-century developments in the economic and political life of our nation and the world, in which we Americans now play a major role."[13] Radical rightists have saturated themselves with false propaganda until fear destroys their ability to deal with the real problems of the day.

Symptoms of paranoia abound in the life of the extremist. He is suspicious of almost everyone and afraid of some evil conspiracy. Suspicion and fear cause him to avoid others. He fears being close to anyone. Wayne Oates wisely says that "a comparative respect for this fear of closeness must be built into our approach to the extremist, for he will not be changed in this respect."[14]

In 1963, Senator Thomas H. Kuchel indicated that he received from one to two hundred letters per day which he described as "fright mail." He said:

> I have, in the past, attempted to reply calmly and factually to "fright mail," mustering all the reason and reserve I could summon . . . for most fright mail writers will come right back a week later, terrified about something else, urgently stating that they do not believe me—and that I am either misinformed or worse.[15]

Senator Kuchel described the extremists of the radical right this way:

> Clutching at half-truths and downright falsehoods, the fright peddlers fabricate hoaxes, as we have seen, which frighten Americans and divert their attention from the real menace. They sow suspicion and hatred. They attempt to undermine faith in Government, its institutions, and its leaders. They preach resistance to the laws of our land. They degrade America and Americans, and do it as well as—or better than—the Communists do.[16]

---

[13] Arnold Forster & Benjamin R. Epstein, *Danger on the Right* (New York: Random House, 1964), p. xviii.

[14] Oates, *op. cit.*, p. 53.

[15] Forster & Epstein, *op. cit.*, p. 48.

[16] *Ibid.*, pp. 48-49.

Those are strong words concerning those who often parade as superpatriots. It is interesting to note that extremists, both left and right, preach resistance to the laws of the land.

Fundamentalists such as Gerald L. K. Smith have long used the scare technique. The author of *Apostles of Discord* described

> ... Smith's constant reference to ubiquitous enemies who are preparing to pounce upon any genuine exponent of Christian Americanism.... Nearly every message from Smith contains mysterious suggestions. He writes vaguely about sinister plots, strange deaths, secret meetings, imminent bloodshed.[17]

Fred Schwarz uses a similar thrust, but it clearly is the communist conspiracy that he fears. Forster and Epstein present a good picture of Schwarz's followers:

> These citizens are not crackpots and malcontents, nor are they lonely, frustrated individuals looking to join about anything that meets and screams. Because of their high educational and income status, most of them are active members of all kinds of church, civic, and veterans' organizations.[18]

Many of his followers may be "solid citizens," but they appear to be motivated by anxiety and fear, and their fear is based on a questionable assessment of the communist threat. Their fear paralyzes them so that they are unable to deal effectively with real threats. They appear to do little more than read books and raise money.

Radical rightists fear many things, and some change their target from time to time. The seventh annual rally of conservative Americans met in Boston in July, 1969. The rally was billed as the "New England Rally for God, Family and Country." It is quite difficult to criticize and oppose people who are rallying for God, family, and country. Such protective coloration is characteristic of extremism. John Fenton reported on the Boston meeting that "the emphasis on the dangers of public sex

[17] Roy, *op. cit.*, pp. 68, 69.
[18] Forster & Epstein, *op. cit.*, p. 59.

education this year replaced the campaign of previous years for the impeachment of Earl Warren, chief justice of the United States, who retired last month."19 Extreme conservatives have warned against such things as fluoridation, social security, coddling labor unions, income tax, and now public sex education. Always the warning is intended to generate fear.

We should recognize that proper fear, well grounded, is a legitimate motivation. There *are* Marxists and communists in America today, and they *do* seek to capitalize on all divisions that develop. And they will advance, encourage, and participate in acts of social revolution.

> Michael Klonsky, national secretary of SDS—the top official—told his organization's national committee at Austin, Tex., on March 30: "Our primary task is to build a Marxist-Leninist revolutionary movement." ... SDS tactics have changed from protest to outright resistance. ... The SDS is generally regarded as the extreme wing of what has come to be known as "the New Left." 20

We need to recognize that there is danger both in the New Left and in the radical right. And we should make sure that fear of neither extreme is permitted to paralyze us in meeting the real issues of our time. Nor should we overreact to the phenomenon of extremism. We must be careful lest we become so obsessed with extremism that we are incapable of bringing about needed social change.

New-found Identity

Possibly it should be noted that some of our citizens are motivated by joy in a new-found identity. And they may behave as extremists at times.

Karl Olsson states that "a people deprived for centuries of the right to think of themselves as having full stature before God; a people forced to survive by being either obsequiously pleasant or criminally 'outside' are

[19] John H. Fenton, "Sex Education Scored at Rally," *The Atlanta Constitution*, Monday, July 7, 1969, p. 38.
[20] *U. S. News & World Report*, May 12, 1969, p. 34.

PSYCHOLOGICAL DIMENSIONS OF EXTREMISM

beginning to see themselves as fully human and are exulting in the beauty of their identity."21 Their exultation may well explode in extremist behavior at times.

Many black-skinned people no longer want to be called Negroes. "The Negro's self-concept may be caricaturized as that of a black-skinned person who desires to be like all other full-fledged Americans (who incidentally are white)."22 The concept of Black Power means to black people something quite different than it does to whites. Nathan Wright says:

> Our black youth, and many of our black professionals, began to recognize that they were not like other full-fledged Americans who happened to be white. Nor could or should they be so. They began to realize that they could take into a common humanity only their own unique black integrity. So it was that "blackness" at least in widespread form was born.23

The black revolution in America is real, and we shall not understand it until we understand the concept of Black Power which black people say was born in the joy of a new-found identity. It is not the purpose of this discussion to deal with the race problem, but we need to recognize that there is a kind of extremism that is motivated by joy in the new identity of blackness. It is a joy that shouts, "Black is beautiful." And some want to withdraw into their cult of blackness.

There is a sense in which sudden wealth also has produced a new identity for some Americans, and it often has resulted in extremism. Wealth has come quickly to some Americans in a number of different ways, but in every case it has thrown people into a new world, formerly unknown to them. And they, too, are exulting in a new-found identity. Brooks Walker, writing in the *Christian Advocate*, stated that "most of the supporters of the fundamentalist right wing are to be found among

---

21 *Proceedings*, p. 9.

22 Nathan Wright, Jr., "The Ethics of Power and the Black Revolution," unpublished presentation to the American Society of Christian Ethics, January 26, 1969, p. 6.

23 *Ibid.*

the newer, but anxious arrivals on the middle-class scene."²⁴ It is possible that such people are motivated more by fear of losing their new-found status than by joy in a new-found identity.

Some who have felt left out and unimportant have found a sense of identity in certain extremist groups. Brooks Walker states that it is a rather touching thing to see "a human personality wanting to be someone, something—anyone, anything at all. But to be real, to have an ego, a sense of purpose." He tells of an anticommunist who said, "The American public is so uninformed. If you know anything at all, you feel like a wizard. It's a tremendous ego builder."²⁵

Although new-found identity is perhaps not itself a psychological dimension of extremism, yet it provides occasion for the development of extremism.

Anarchic Totalitarianism

Harry and Bonaro Overstreet refer to the fact that radical rightism is called both anarchic and fascist. They object:

> Neither term fits the complex actuality; and we have found none that does. Our current choice, till we find a better, is *anarchic totalitarianism*—which is self-contradictory enough to cover both the Rightists' fierce objection to being controlled in any way and their readiness to control and coerce others by all expedient means.²⁶

Certainly, the extremist is a cultist. The Overstreets state, for example, that radical rightism "fosters the cult of the Leader, reducing the rank-and-file to a kind of task force to carry out directives and exert pressures at assigned points."²⁷ The frustrated, authoritarian personality finds security under the wing of the authoritari-

---

²⁴ Brooks R. Walker, "Sources of the Radical Right," *Christian Advocate*, August 27, 1964, p. 9.

²⁵ *Ibid.*

²⁶ Harry and Bonaro Overstreet, *The Strange Tactics of Extremism* (New York: W. W. Norton, 1964), p. 268.

²⁷ *Ibid.*

an leader or organization. Wayne Oates states that "the authoritarian personality has unconscious dependency needs and leans heavily upon the 'ones above' him.... In an authoritarian society, he depends heavily on the leader."[28] Extremists are more secure when they carry out orders, when they identify with an authoritarian person—the leader. They are very sensitive to criticism and are not effective on the defensive. This is true of both the leader and the follower.

Extremist leaders are characterized by an authoritarianism that often indicates a kind of messianic complex. Referring to the letters of Gerald L. K. Smith, the author of *Apostles of Discord* says that "he concludes with a humble assurance that Gerald L. K. Smith will battle on, even in the face of death or imprisonment. 'If my enemies could do it without unfavorable reaction, I would be murdered or imprisoned within a week.' "[29] Fred Schwarz has been characterized by one of his employees as "a fussy autocrat." Employees say that he "sees himself as incapable of error and is thus intolerant of the mistakes of others."[30] The symptoms of paranoia are easily recognized in such leaders, who are afflicted with a persecution complex and delusions of grandeur.

Possibly none surpassed J. Frank Norris as an authoritarian leader, and his was the cult of fundamentalism. Ralph Roy states that "to his enemies he was a 'self-centered tyrant' with a flair for publicity."[31] Of his extremist, authoritarian method Roy says:

> Norris launched into a scurrilous smear campaign against all those who resisted his iron hand. He charged them with every form of vice, including financial manipulations, marital infidelity, sexual perversion, and religious racketeering. Most of these attacks were vividly portrayed in *Fundamentalist* cartoons.[32]

[28] Oates, *op. cit.*, p. 42.
[29] Roy, *op. cit.*, p. 69.
[30] Forster & Epstein, *op. cit.*, p. 54.
[31] Roy, *op. cit.*, p. 351.
[32] *Ibid.*, p. 356.

The cultic group recognizes no authority but its own. All other authorities become targets for attacks. This was demonstrated well in the case of J. Frank Norris. He and his followers were almost constantly attacking George W. Truett, the great patriarch of Southern Baptists. In fact, few Southern Baptist leaders escaped their attack.

Some leaders of the radical right are really insecure people, although they stand as strong, authoritarian leaders. This appears to be true of Fred Schwarz. Some who know him "report that despite his air of self-confidence Schwarz is a nervous man who seems insecure, and that when unsure of himself he either bites his fingernails or cracks his knuckles."[33]

There is probably a bit of authoritarian extremism in most of us. Wayne Oates observes, "Both you and I have a built-in propensity to think of ourselves as the center and lord of things, both geographically and ideologically."[34] Everyone's ego needs feeding. We may well discover our own tendencies toward extremism as we try to deal with extremism.

A bit of humility might serve us well in coming to grips with anarchic authoritarianism. "The psychological mechanism of projection operates overtime in the extremist."[35] We need to exercise care that we do not try to escape our own responsibility by projecting blame on extremists for all of our social ills.

Conclusion

Extremism is a sickness that will not be cured until lines of communication can be established with the extremists. Much more effort is needed in seeking to communicate with extremists of both left and right. Achieving a climate of free discussion with them will require little less than a miracle. But such a climate is essential if attitudes are to be changed.

[33] Forster & Epstein, *op. cit.*, p. 54.
[34] Oates, *op. cit.*, p. 37.
[35] *Ibid.*, p. 39.

We should not anticipate any real improvement until we are willing to listen as well as be heard, or until we are through with name-calling. Denouncing extremism with clever terms may be great sport for some and entertaining to others, but it weakens even further the lines of communication. We should search for common concerns that will provide for true communication.

There is but a thin line between the true prophet and the extremist. The prophets of God will find it necessary to stand outside the organized church or in an uncomfortable position within the organized church. They will be viewed by many as extremists. It has ever been so. But the true prophet will not be an extremist in the sense that we have defined extremism. The attitudes and motivations of the prophet will be quite different from those of the extremist. His life will be characterized by faith, not fear; hope, not frustration; love, not hatred.

To the loyal, concerned, prophetic Christian who is beset with rumors and false accusations, Jesus said:

> Blessed are ye, when men shall revile you, and persecute you, and shall say all manner of evil against you falsely, for my sake. Rejoice, and be exceeding glad: for great is your reward in heaven: for so persecuted they the prophets which were before you (Matthew 5:11-12).

We should strive to overcome intolerance and hatred with tolerance and love. We should strive to conquer fear with faith. And where we find division, we should seek to be ambassadors of reconciliation. It is to this kind of ministry that we have been called, and we should be satisfied with nothing less.

6

Tactics of Extremists

John C. Howell

Thus far in our discussions of extremism we have learned something of the nature of extremism and of the groups which comprise the right and left wings of the movement in our society. Now we turn our attention to the tactics used by extremists in their attempts to influence the American people. Victor C. Ferkiss underscores the importance of this phase of our study in his observation that the distinctive characteristic of extremist groups in America "is not so much the express content of their ideas as their methods, the nature of their appeal to their followers, and their inability to accommodate their goals to those of the dominant consensus."[1]

In view of the different emphases being promoted by the left- and right-wing groups, it may seem unfair to discuss both ends of the spectrum in the same general terms. However, the study of their methodology leads one to accept the position of *Look* editor George B. Leonard that "beneath the deception of surface appearances, extremists of the Right and Left are startlingly

---

[1] Victor C. Ferkiss, "Political and Intellectual Origins of American Radicalism, Right and Left," *The Annals of the American Academy of Political and Social Science*, November, 1962, p. 2.

John C. Howell is Professor of Christian Ethics, Midwestern Baptist Theological Seminary, Kansas City, Missouri.

similar."[2] The similarities, and the differences, will become more evident as we continue our investigation into their methodology.

As the story unfolds, you may find yourself asking, "How can intelligent people who are supposedly devoted to their country do such things to other people?" Part of the answer to this question is that threats loom so large in the eyes of extremists that they will try any method deemed necessary to overcome the threat. Ferkiss concisely expresses the extremist perspective:

> If the threat is universal and absolute, then all anti-Communist measures are justified. Secrecy, infiltration, and calumny—established Communist methods—must be used against them; because their agents are everywhere—in universities, on school boards, in Congress—then the methods can be used anywhere.[3]

Such paranoia enables individuals to justify unchristian and undemocratic action, just as mass hysteria can lead to crowd behavior which each individual would repudiate in a more rational frame of mind.

With this introduction to the meaning of tactics and methods for extremists, let us now identify some of the weapons used in their battle against the moderate middle.

Tactics

(1) Polarize issues in oversimplified categories

Most guilty in this regard is the radical right, which polarizes every issue in the framework of a communist conspiracy! The left does not center its polemic against American society around one fundamental issue, but it tends to advance simple solutions to complex issues. The theme, "Make love, not war," sounds good but offers no constructive way of coping with the political problem of war. Jack Newfield, in his sympathetic study

---

[2] George B. Leonard, "What Is an Extremist?", *Look*, October 20, 1964, p. 35.

[3] Ferkiss, *op. cit.*, p. 10.

of the New Left, aptly comments that the followers of the movement "are sometimes hopelessly romantic, especially about unromantic aberrations like violence and authoritarianism."[4]

The menace of communism from within is the constant theme of many right-wing organizations. In *The Blue Book of the John Birch Society*, Robert Welch has set forth in concrete terms the argument that runs through the propaganda of all these groups.

> As I see it, I am afraid you have just two alternatives. Either you, and tens of thousands like you, come into the John Birch Society and, without giving it the whole of your lives, still devote to its purposes the best and most you can offer, with money and head and heart as well as hand; or in a very few years you will, by force, be devoting *all* to the maintenance of a Communist slave state.[5]

According to the propaganda of the Minutemen this hour has already arrived: "You are now living in a Communist-occupied territory!"[6]

For the militant left, the major issues are the Vietnam War, racism, and the depersonalization of life by the Establishment. The last term may refer to the huge university, the affluent society, the technological orientation of life, or the military-industrial complex. The New Left, which Newfield distinguishes from the older, Marxist-oriented movements, wants to turn back the clock of political-economic development to a point where each person gains more meaningful personal experiences. Such a new society requires "participatory democracy" where the will of the small and forgotten individual has more weight than in today's complex society. In suggesting ways of accomplishing this goal, many followers of the movement naively suggest "that through sincere and determined organizing the people's essential goodness will transform itself into effective

[4] Jack Newfield, *A Prophetic Minority* (New York: New American Library, 1966), p. 17.
[5] *The Blue Book of the John Birch Society* (Sixteenth printing; Belmont, Mass.: Western Islands, 1961), p. 161.
[6] Leonard, *op. cit.*, p. 33.

politics."⁷ But it is possible that participation in social action movements may help them develop a more practical political approach.

(2) Create hysteria and fear

Perhaps as a consequence of their mingling of religion with anticommunism, many right-wing leaders proclaim their message of fear with evangelistic fervor. When Fred Schwarz of The Christian Anti-Communism Crusade warned an audience of the time "when they come for you . . . on a dark night, in a dark cellar, and they take a wide bore revolver with a soft nose bullet, and they place it at the nape of your neck . . . ,"⁸ the element of fear in his message was clear.

Rumor, insinuation, and exhortation help create fear among the adherents of the right, and they are also evident in the extremist left when dissident students and dissatisfied blacks threaten reprisals against those who stand in the way of their idea of progress. Probably the best example of mass hysteria generated by extremists centered on the Water Moccasin III exercise in Georgia in 1963.⁹

Water Moccasin III was a U.S. Army field operation intended to train officers and men in guerrilla combat. An enemy force (of U.S. personnel) was to attack "Claxtonia," a simulated country at Fort Stewart, and a counter-guerrilla force (of U.S. personnel) was to try to stop the aggressors. In addition, 124 foreign officers who had attended the same combat school as the U.S. officers were to be involved. Civilians from Claxton, Georgia, were also invited to share in certain phases of the exercise and willingly agreed to do so.

The Texas Voters for Enforcing the Constitution were reportedly first to identify the exercise as a United Nations plot to plant foreign troops on American soil

⁷ Paul Jacobs and Saul Landau, *The New Radicals: A Report with Documents* (New York: Vintage Books, 1966), p. 38.

⁸ Quoted in "The Radical Right and Religion," *The Anti-Defamation League Christian Friends*, September, 1965, pp. 3-4.

⁹ Leonard, *op. cit.*, pp. 35-37.

under the control of a Russian general. The rumor spread quickly, and gained more and more embellishments. Congressman James B. Utt of California wrote in a report to his constituents:

> We do not know whether African troops will be involved or not, but we do know that there is a large contingent of barefooted Africans that have been moved into Cuba for training in guerrilla warfare. . . .
>
> Who brought these Africans to Cuba? Was it the United Nations? Was it Russia? Or was it the United States?

Congressman Utt's letter was reprinted and circulated by the Keep America Committee in Los Angeles, then distributed throughout the nation by The Network of Patriotic Letter Writers.

Hysterical reactions to this rumor campaign deluged congressmen, local newspapers, and radio stations. The Army finally backed down and cancelled plans for civilian participation. But the rumors did not cease. In March, the Americans United Council in Long Beach, California, warned the faithful of imminent peril in Georgia:

> *Your Country, your Native Land—the United States of America—has just been invaded by military troops of foreign lands!* . . .
>
> Advices come from Maryland, Georgia, South Carolina, Texas, Washington, D.C. Here are quotes:. . . .
>
> "AFRICANS LANDING IN SAVANNAH (Georgia). Advance contingent of the UNITED NATIONS combat troops of Ghana and India from Katanga duty . . . . As many negro troops as others . . . ."

The affair finally died down in the national press, but it is still mentioned in rightist literature as one time when violent right-wing reaction prevented the government from selling out America to the United Nations. The whole affair was a hoax created by rumor and hysteria, but the rightists still believe it was a communist plot.

(3) Foster distrust of leadership

Another tactic used regularly by right and left alike is undermining trust in the leadership of government, religion, business, educational agencies, and national organizations. For example, several sources claim that seven thousand Protestant clergymen are involved in communist front activities, but no proof is given. Billy James Hargis went even farther in 1961 when he declared, "Eighty-two hundred Protestant ministers have joined Communist fronts since the 1930's."[10] Even though no evidence is given, such statements create distrust of ministers and denominational leaders in a way that cannot be resisted effectively. Rev. Gilbert C. Murphy, pastor of the Gardner Presbyterian Church near Kansas City, pinpointed the problem: "If some of us are Communists, I wish someone would call us Communists as individuals so we could take it into court and get it straightened out!"[11]

The National Parent-Teacher Association has also been attacked by radical rightists who claim it pressures members into conformity with its communist-inspired activities. In response to this attack, the National PTA prepared an excellent pamphlet describing the tactics of extremism and indicating how local groups can resist their attempt to take over the group.

One of the most damaging tactics of the extremist right has been to accuse United States Presidents, congressmen, and judges of being either active communist agents or dupes of the communist line. Revilo P. Oliver, professor of classics at the University of Illinois, made the incredible accusation that President John F. Kennedy was a communist who was falling behind in delivering the assigned quota of conspiratorial gains for the party. Consequently he was assassinated by the communists, who succeeded in placing the blame on American

---

[10] Kansas City *Star*, July 23, 1961.
[11] Kansas City *Star*, February 4, 1962.

patriots and thus slowing down the development of resistance to communism in America.[12]

Distrust is created, therefore, by misrepresentation, blacklisting, and distortion of the truth. The Overstreets point out that the "problem of coping with Radical Rightist materials is, in major degree, a problem of learning how each leader characteristically makes words and phrases do his bidding: how he makes them conduct the reader's mind to the conclusion that he wants it to reach."[13] Thus when Schwarz or Hargis declares that communists are infiltrating churches and government without offering proof of his statements, he creates strong suspicion even though he may never document his charges.

(4) Coerce and intimidate dissenters

School and public librarians, newspaper editors, local pastors, and elected legislators have learned that resistance to extremist groups can bring immediate and violent reaction. Economic boycott is also used as a means of coercion. This was vividly demonstrated by D. B. Lewis, president of Lewis Food Company, who sponsored Dan Smoot on radio and television. When a California newspaper defended the United Nations, supported President Kennedy's social programs, and criticized the radical right, its Lewis Food Company advertisements were cancelled. The explanation given was: "Mr. Lewis is spending so much money promoting Conservative causes that he doesn't want to dilute his efforts."[14]

Name-calling is another form of intimidation used to run down the opposition. Anyone who criticizes the radical right is likely to be publicly branded a communist sympathizer.

---

[12] Revilo P. Oliver, "Marksmanship: In Dallas," *American Opinion*, February, 1964.

[13] Harry and Bonaro Overstreet, *The Strange Tactics of Extremism* (New York: W. W. Norton, 1964), pp. 187-188.

[14] Arnold Forster and Benjamin R. Epstein, *Danger on the Right* (New York: Random House, 1964), p. 140.

(5) Infiltrate existing organizations and gain control

When Minuteman Troy Haughton was interviewed by a *Look* editor, he emphasized the organization's use of infiltration tactics. "We still practice guerrilla tactics," he remarked, "but for the last year, we've stressed infiltrating into Left-Wing or peace organizations by people who are not known as Rightists."[15]

This means of influencing organizations is directly in line with the directive laid down by Robert Welch in the September, 1960, issue of the John Birch Society *Bulletin*. He instructed Society members to "join your local PTA at the beginning of the school year, get your conservative friends to do likewise, and go to work to take it over." After becoming active members, they should seek to be elected to positions of leadership, particularly in program planning, and attempt to turn the organization into a forum for rightist ideas.

A familiar right-wing tactic noted by the National PTA is that of prolonging meetings until most of the other delegates have left and then passing resolutions which support their position. Another is to plant people in mass meetings to harass the speakers with loaded, unanswerable questions and create confusion.

The left wing is also using infiltration to gain control of existing organizations. For example, the communist desire to move into the student movement is reflected in an interview by Thomas Powers of United Press International with Ken Wallach of Columbia University's Russian Institute: "In the next couple of years I expect to see at least 2,000 radical students join the party," he said. "I also expect an equal number of young factory workers."[16]

(6) Organize front groups with patriotic names

An estimated five to seven million Americans belong to organizations and movements of the far left and far

---

[15] Leonard, *op. cit.*, p. 34.
[16] *The Denver Post*, August 10, 1969, p. 13.

right. The left has organized such groups as Students for a Democratic Society (SDS), Student Nonviolent Coordinating Committee (SNCC), and Free Speech Movement. The right has tended to form ranks behind more nationalistic labels such as The Patrick Henry Society, Defenders of the American Constitution, and Liberty Lobby. The similarity between the names of rightist groups and those of other legitimate organizations striving for a better America often confuses people who receive literature from extremist groups without knowing anything about their program.

(7) Develop propaganda outlets

The ten-point program advocated by Robert Welch in section four of *The Blue Book* recommends establishing reading rooms or lending libraries in as many communities as possible to distribute books and literature carefully selected by the society. These would serve as indoctrination centers to promote the extremist viewpoint. He also suggests starting book stores where such materials are the main items of trade. In the Kansas City area the Freedom Center Book Store is the main such outlet, although some other dealers handle this material in conjunction with conservative religious books and supplies.

Placing periodicals such as *National Review, Human Events, The Dan Smoot Report,* and *American Opinion* in strategic places—doctors' offices, barber shops, and other places where people spend time waiting—is another form of propaganda distribution.

A more intensive program of spreading the tenets of extremism, however, is accomplished through films and speakers made available to various organizations in the community. In 1962 the Boy Scouts' Kansas City Area Council was showing and making available the Birch-sponsored filmstrip "Communism on the Map," and it was the only visual aid they had dealing with communism. After widespread criticism by area leaders it was withdrawn, but it remained available through the Council's office for some time.

The Overstreets point out that the Communist Party USA also provides speakers for meetings. From its New York office "it is engaged in an all-out effort to secure speaking engagements for top-ranking Party members—with student and church audiences as prime targets."[17]

Whenever leaders feel a need for stirring up a community over a particularly important issue, competent speakers from the national office are ready to go anywhere in the United States for speaking engagements that can result in community action. Dr. Gordon Drake of the Christian Crusade has traveled across the country arousing opposition to sex education programs in the public schools.

Another kind of propaganda activity is the organized letter-writing campaign. The John Birch Society has often utilized this strategy, as have other extremist groups.

(8) Appeal for money to fight the enemy

Wayne Oates rightly observes that "the extremist is characterized by commercialism . . . . They keep the hurrah going because it is profitable to them."[18] Examples can be drawn from most of the radical right groups; one classic illustration was Billy James Hargis' fundraising campaign at the Annual Convention of the Christian Crusade in Tulsa on August 3, 1969. Having broken ground for a patriotic school to be known as American College, Hargis announced the need for funds to build a dormitory and began appealing for contributions.

> "Dear God," Hargis prayed, at the start of his plea, "young people can go to so few schools that champion conservative principles and Americanist ideas, may we see tonight the necessity of putting to work what we have while we're still alive.
>
> "Oh, precious Jesus, our hearts are breaking over the paths so many of our youths are taking . . . .

[17] H. and B. Overstreet, *op. cit.*, p. 110.
[18] Wayne Oates, "Southern Baptists and Extremism," *Baptist Program*, September, 1965, p. 3.

"I need $35,000. I need some big gifts. Not only for the school, but for all the things we're doing."[19]

The appeal netted $70,000, including one gift of $25,000.

This effort was similar to Hargis's appeal to the third annual convention, when he raised $38,870 to purchase radio time on the Mutual Broadcasting System. Forster and Epstein commented then that the "entire proceeding was, in short, an auction by a skilled performer who was selling God, religion, the church, and the preservation of the United States while he held the Bible in one hand and a cash register in the other."[20]

Hargis told reporters at the Tulsa meeting that the Christian Crusade's annual budget exceeds two million dollars, the bulk of the income coming from direct mail solicitations sent to a mailing list of two hundred thousand.

These are some of the tactics extremist groups use to fulfill their goals of indoctrinating Americans and influencing them to adopt their views. Let us now look briefly at two examples of these tactics in action.

Examples

(1) Harvard and the New Left

Harvard University long prided itself on its ability to settle extreme differences of opinion peaceably. In April, 1969, however, Harvard joined the ranks of U.S. universities which have felt the shock of attack by leftist organizations, particularly SDS.

SDS, along with SNCC, is usually considered one of the major forces of the New Left. It was formally founded in June, 1962, at Port Huron, Michigan, by fifty-five young people from eleven functioning chapters. Its loosely developed program includes opposition to militarism, bureaucracy, the Vietnam War, and anticommunism as practiced by the radical right (even

[19] Kansas City *Times*, August 4, 1969.
[20] Forster and Epstein, *op. cit.*, p. 73.

TACTICS OF EXTREMISTS

though it is also opposed to communist domination of the individual). SDS pledges support for the underprivileged, particularly in the ghetto.

The conflict at Harvard, reported *Time* magazine, was led by about 250 students from Harvard and Radcliffe, "most of them members of Students for a Democratic Society and the pro-Mao Progressive Labor Party."[21] The main issues were the abolition of ROTC on campus and the end of what was called Harvard's expansionist attitude toward its urban neighbors. ROTC, in the protesters' eyes, symbolized the partnership of the University with the military establishment, and the expansion of Harvard's physical plant was condemned for displacing the urban poor without their consent.

After reading their demands for action, the radical students took over University Hall, the administration building which housed the five deans of the university. Physically expelling one of the deans, the students locked themselves in the building.

Early the next morning, by order of President Nathan M. Pusey, state and local police entered Harvard Yard. The dissident students were given five minutes to vacate the building and then were forcibly ejected by the police.

The effects of Pusey's use of police, however, were felt during the next week as students and faculty held meetings to consider the situation. The students voted a strike, and the faculty voted not to support President Pusey's use of police without prior consultation.

Time commented that "neither students, faculty nor administration could claim a clear-cut victory in the Harvard strike,"[22] but the strike did demonstrate the power of the radical left as a catalyst for institutional policy change.

Tactically, SDS dramatized issues by polarization, flooded the campus with 750,000 mimeographed propaganda leaflets, disrupted classes, and forced the discussion of issues by all areas of academic life. The

[21] *Time*, April 18, 1969, p. 47.
[22] *Time*, April 25, 1969, p. 45.

Harvard situation seems a clear application of "The Port Huron Statement" upon which SDS was founded:

> The significance of these scattered movements lies not in their success or failure in gaining objectives—at least not yet.... The significance is in the fact that the students are breaking the crust of apathy and overcoming the inner alienation that remain the defining characteristics of American college life.[23]

(2) Sex education and the radical right

In the January, 1969, issue of the John Birch Society *Bulletin*, members were informed that they must give "organized, nationwide, intensive, *angry* and determined opposition to the now mushrooming program of so-called sex education in the public schools." After describing the extent of plans for such education, the article declared that a "preponderant majority of the American people are not yet even aware of this filthy Communist plot, of the tremendous drive that is behind it, or of its triple significance."

Members of the right wing are being encouraged to form MOTOREDE (Movement to Restore Decency) Committees in their communities to arouse resistance to sex education in the schools because "the sex educators are in league with sexologists—who represent every shade of muddy gray morality, ministers colored atheistic pink, and camp followers of every persuasion—offbeat psychiatrists to ruthless publishers of pornography."[24]

The attack has been focused on the Sex Information and Education Council of the United States (SIECUS) board members and executive secretary. They are accused of communist leanings and immoral attitudes toward sexual expression among young people and adults. The familiar tactics of name-calling and guilt by association are used extensively, and examples of bad teaching are used to create anxiety among parents.

[23] Jacobs and Landau, *op. cit.*, p. 157.
[24] Gordon V. Drake, *Is the School House the Place to Teach Raw Sex?* (Tulsa: Christian Crusade Publications, 1968), p. 31.

Some board members of SIECUS do represent viewpoints on sexual ethics which most of us would find objectionable, but their view is not that of the board as a whole.

Sex education is sometimes opposed because it is reported to be simply an experience in pornography, an exercise in license, or an exposure of kindergarten children to sexual intercourse through visual aids. It is true that a few teachers have made irresponsible use of available materials, but many of the rumors about bad teaching bear little resemblance to reality.

One example of such misrepresentation is found in much of the literature opposed to public sexual education. A teacher in Lansing, Michigan, it is claimed, "intending to illustrate a point under discussion, removes all her clothing in front of her class."[25]

Dr. Luther G. Baker, Jr., Professor of Family Life at Central Washington State College, wrote to the Michigan school involved to determine the facts of this case. He learned that a physical education teacher "was attempting to demonstrate to her all-girl class how differently-constructed garments affect perceptions of the human figure. She brought several dresses to class, and changing into the different styles discussed the subtle meanings which attach to clothing and the manner in which it is worn." At no time did the teacher remove all of her clothing before the class.[26]

One leader of this fight is Dr. Gordon V. Drake, educational director for the Christian Crusade. His book, *Is the School House the Proper Place to Teach Raw Sex?*, though it is filled with misquotes and distortions of fact, has been distributed by the thousands throughout the country and accepted as the true story of public school sexual education.

Drake specializes in going into communities where sexual education programs are under consideration to arouse right-wing opposition. In November, 1968, he

[25] "Sex Education: Assault on American Youth," *American Education Lobby*, 1969, p. 1.
[26] "The Rising Furor over Sex Education," reprint by Kansas City Social Health Society, 1969.

visited Kansas City to help the Concerned Parents Committee raise funds to oppose programs in the Kansas and Missouri school systems. Members of the local John Birch Society had utilized his materials earlier in the year to disrupt a community meeting; the speaker at that meeting said later that she had never seen such hate in people's eyes as she did that night.

In March, 1969, Drake traveled to Nashville, Tennessee to speak to a MOTOREDE-sponsored assembly. His appearance was scheduled one night prior to a public hearing on sex education plans for the Nashville schools and led the *Nashville Banner* to criticize the proposed plan sharply. The ensuing controversy drew a sharp rebuke to sex education opponents from Mrs. W. E. Miller, president of the Council of Parent-Teacher Associations: "Much of this literature is nothing but irresponsible, venomous, and sometimes libelous attacks on individuals and organizations."[27] It also brought a resolution by Metro Councilman James L. Warren to keep sex education out of the schools, but the Council refused to accept this action. Later a Parents' Committee to keep sexual education in the home was formed and the Metro Board of Education promised to have public hearings on any sex education plan proposed for the schools.

The right of parents to determine what their children will be taught about sex is an important right and needs to be guarded. However, the methods of extremists would destroy the excellent work being done in family life education in many school systems while spewing out hate literature attributing such education programs to a communist conspiracy. In the May, 1969, *Bulletin* of the John Birch Society, Robert Welch exults in the *Wall Street Journal's* report on the poll taken by Oakland television station KTVU. Viewers were asked, "Is sex education a communist plot?" and 703 of 1,385 persons who called in said yes. Welch commented, "And for that most encouraging growth of public understanding we do claim a lot of credit."[28]

[27] Quoted in Nashville *Tennessean*, April 1, 1969, p. 2.
[28] John Birch Society *Bulletin*, May, 1969, p. 11.

7

Extremists and the Mass Media

Thomas A. Bland

The mass media of communication in present-day America are mirrors of our culture and shapers of our way of life. As mirrors the mass media reflect what is happening to us. As shapers the media play a prominent role in determining, or attempting to determine, what will happen to us.

As mirrors and as shapers the mass media are vulnerable targets for extremism. If extremism is basically an individual or group reaction against threat, as Professor Oates has said,[1] the mass media provide opportunities to observe both individual and group reactions at work.

This chapter will attempt to do five things: (1) to show the importance of the mass media in contemporary American life; (2) to review and summarize the processes and effects of communication through the mass media, showing ways in which the mass media are exploited by extremists for their purposes; (3) to review briefly the ways in which the Democratic National Convention of 1968 was dealt with in the mass media, with the purpose of showing how the media were used

[1] Wayne E. Oates, *Pastoral Counseling in Social Problems* (Philadelphia: Westminster Press, 1966), p. 37.

Thomas A. Bland is Professor of Christian Ethics and Sociology, Southeastern Baptist Theological Seminary, Wake Forest, North Carolina.

by left-wingers, in particular, including some leftist extremists; (4) to document, not exhaustively but by way of illustration, how right-wing groups employ the mass media; and (5) to offer some suggestions of ways to deal with extremism as it is manifested through the mass media of communication.

Importance of the Mass Media

In the late twentieth century in the United States, we are far along in the revolution in communications. The variety of the media of communication is growing. Methods of communication are expanding and undergoing constant refinement. The impact of the mass media is phenomenal.

Newspapers, magazines, radio, and television comprise the major categories of the media. One of every three Americans buys or subscribes to a daily newspaper. Undoubtedly, most of these newspapers are shared with others. Consequently the readership is extremely high, the most reliable estimate being that more than 110 million Americans read a daily newspaper. Nearly 600 million magazines are circulated annually. Three billion dollars are taken in from book sales each year. More than half a billion books, excluding textbooks, are bought each year in the United States.

Radio and television, the former emphasizing auditory perception and the latter effectively combining visual and auditory communication, are virtually omnipresent in our culture. Ninety-eight percent of the homes in America have radios, and more than 86 percent have television sets. There are more than 800 television stations in the United States and in excess of 3,200 radio stations.

One index of the impact of the mass media is the time devoted to them by the average American. It has been said that "a reasonable guess" is that the average American devotes thirty-five hours per week to the mass media, with television's share of this time growing ever larger.[2] These figures, it should be pointed out, repre-

[2] Kyle Haselden, *Morality and the Mass Media* (Nashville: Broadman Press, 1968), p. 59.

sent approximately 15 percent of the total time available, a period nearly equal to that given to one's job and ten times what a church member in regular attendance gives to his church.

Polls indicate that for two thirds of present-day Americans television is the primary source of news. Walter Cronkite, Eric Sevareid, Howard K. Smith, Paul Harvey, and others are immensely popular, powerful dispensers and interpreters of news.

One insightful specialist, a journalist-editor who is also a distinguished Southern Baptist deacon, Mr. Warner B. Ragsdale, Sr., has written: "The impact of the media upon public attitudes reaches fantastic proportions. It far exceeds that of all the schools, universities, churches, and books in the land."[3]

Without lingering too long on the obvious pervasiveness of the impact of mass communications, some further historical documentation seems appropriate.

In a discriminating article, Dean W. C. Clark of the School of Journalism of Syracuse University has shown that much of the social legislation that affects our lives today can be credited to the mass media. Professor Clark further notes that the media have not been given adequate credit. For example, social historians credit the Social Security Act, with its far-reaching benefits and aids, to the New Deal of President Franklin Delano Roosevelt and the small band of brain-trusters who worked with him. Clark notes, however, that, for seventy-five years before the New Deal, the insurance companies in this nation had, through the mass media, been advocating a guarantee of security in old age. To be sure, they were selling insurance, through advertising, in the mass media. Nevertheless, they helped to create the climate and even provided the slogans for Social Security legislation.

More recently, Medicaid and Medicare have emerged, and they were not created *de novo* and *ex nihilo* by smart politicians. Instead, smart politicians seized upon ideas which had been drummed into the American people for twenty years by the propaganda of various

[3] Quoted from *Report from the Capital*, August, 1969, p. 8.

insurance businesses carried in newspapers, magazines, radio, and television.

The Peace Corps, Clark claims, is not to be credited solely to the political genius of John F. Kennedy. The idea must be credited in large part to mass media's account over a hundred years of the work of Christian missionaries in bettering living conditions of people in underdeveloped countries. Consequently, the Peace Corps began as a kind of secular missionary work.[4]

It is clear from this review that the mass media have a tremendous impact upon the lives of people. This is true on the basis of the numbers of persons reached. It is also true on the basis of the documented evidence of the effect of advertising, reporting, editorializing, and news analysis on the destiny of people, legislation, and national interests.

Mass Media Communication: Process and Effects

"Communication" comes from the Latin word *communicare*, which means "to share," "to impart," "to transmit," "to make common." For communication to occur, therefore, there must be a sender, a receiver, a substance to be communicated, and a vehicle of communication.

Communication begins with an idea or impulse in the sender's mind. This idea is given formal expression as it is encoded and transmitted to the receiver. The process of communication is not complete until the receiver interprets the message through some decoding process. Furthermore, there must be feedback of some kind. This feedback is essential for the completion of one full cycle of communication.

In the process of communication, the receiver's decoding apparatus is very important. All of us have had the experience of receiving feedback which was quite different from what we said, or thought we had said. The reason for this is that the receiver decodes the

[4] W. C. Clark, "The Impact of Mass Communications in America," in *The Annals* of the American Academy of Political and Social Science, vol. 378 (July, 1968), pp. 68-74.

message through psychological and other personal and social "filters." What the receiver actually *hears* is affected by these filters. This fact has special significance in dealing with extremism. For a white supremacist-segregationist, a sermon dealing with the love of God and neighbor is *heard*, interpreted, resented, and resisted as a call for integration.

In mass communication the process described becomes proportionately more complex as the sender is more remote from the receiver, the medium of communication is more impersonal, and the opportunity for feedback is more indirect. For example, the input or content is more likely to gain ready acceptance if it reflects the existing value systems of society. Exploitation of familiar concepts through the employment of language which is in common usage is one technique of effective mass communication. Likewise, an appeal which reaches emotions is more effective than one which is aimed solely or even primarily at reason.

What are some desirable effects of communication through the mass media?

As has been suggested, one desired effect is to get the message across so as to influence behavior in appropriate ways. Obviously, there are times when the most desirable result of public communication would be to strengthen the status quo. To promote and enlarge consensus on basic policies would be one such result. The building of social stability through strengthening majorities against the onslaught of dissident minorities is another. Public administration and national defense are sensitive areas in which, in a democracy, strong public support is crucial.

There are, on the other hand, desirable social changes which can be inaugurated and implemented through the media of mass communication. Changing fashions, fads, or even more basic life styles are cases in point. More significantly, the enlargement or extension of the range of discourse through popularizing new ideas, terms, concepts, and technical or cultural achievements is very worthwhile.

In the realm of politics, in our time, the mass media

have moved discussion of basic issues into ever-enlarging arenas. Partisan politics can no longer be confined to smoke-filled rooms. Basic domestic and international issues are brought from diplomatic and legislative chambers and aired before large, diverse publics. Governments may react by attempting to manage the news or by withholding or distorting information, but in the ensuing credibility gaps the government and its manipulators are most likely to be the ultimate losers.

There are at least three negative factors in the influence of the mass media in political issues. Each of these has a bearing on the subject of this book.

The first negative effect is that many crucial issues are overlooked by the mass media. Inundated by news, the media have reacted by creating higher thresholds of attention. This leads to more selectivity and to greater concentration on national issues, national figures, and selected branches of government, especially the legislative and executive.[5]

The second negative effect is that coverage of political issues has moved from the precision of the rifle to the scattering of the shotgun. With some exceptions, the media have moved away from the specific in the direction of more general issues. The aim is apparently not small group consensus but centralized propaganda.

The third negative effect has been the exposure, primarily through television, of the weaknesses of the national political party conventions. Former President Eisenhower commented unfavorably on the way in which television broadcasts "these riotous proceedings" called nominating conventions in this country and abroad. One of his suggestions was to keep all reporters off the convention floor and provide the media with off-the-floor facilities. Mr. Eisenhower seemed particularly bothered by the image of chaos which he felt was projected from the conventions.[6]

[5] *Ibid.*, p. 73.

[6] Dwight D. Eisenhower, "Our National Nominating Conventions Are a Disgrace," in Francis M. Carney and H. Frank Way, Jr., *Politics, 1968* (Belmont, California: Wadsworth, 1967), pp. 119-123.

On balance, it must be said that two very desirable features of the mass media in the United States are the freedom of expression which they enjoy and the financing of these media by private enterprise. Our pluralistic society not only demands a variety of media but requires that a broad spectrum of materials and emphases be exposed through these media. Private capital, which utilizes advertising and other commercial devices, is the largest financier of all the media of mass communication in this country.

The combination of all these features provides a setting for infiltration, manipulation, and other forms of exploitation of the media by extremists. There has been enough dissent in this nation over the Vietnam War, for example, for the polarization of the American people to be dramatized and also made greater through the mass media. Communism as a threat to the democratic and capitalistic values of the American people is the issue by which some extremist groups have expressed their right-wing viewpoints. Religion is another vital interest which extremists exploit. Despite our historic American traditions of pluralism and freedom of religious expressions, doctrinal emphases, competing forms of religious organization, and a host of pseudo- and quasi-religious concerns provide the umbrella under which intolerance and bigotry are sometimes set before reading, listening, or viewing publics.

Within our system of freedom of communication financed by the private sector, what controls can be placed on extremism's exploitation of the mass media? This question will receive a fuller treatment in the last section of this chapter and in the last chapter of this book. But three suggestions may be briefly noted at this point. First, the media themselves should employ high standards of accuracy, objectivity, fairness in reporting, care in editorializing, and professional ethics in the processes of communication. Secondly, the public's interests, represented in the legal guidelines of such regulatory agencies as the Federal Communications Commission, should be zealously protected. In the third place, an alert, intelligent, ethically sensitive public will provide one of the best controls against extremism in the mass media of communication.

Extremism and the Media at the Democratic National Convention of 1968

For years to come, historians, journalists, and others will probably be interpreting and reinterpreting the events of the Democratic National Convention held in Chicago on August 26-29, 1968. Charges and counter-charges have been made, and will probably continue to be made, against Chicago Mayor Richard Daley, the official leadership of the Democratic National Convention, the various groups of protesters gathered in Chicago, the Chicago police, and the media of mass communication.

I have tried to study this situation as objectively as possible on the basis of written documentation from a number of sources. The events centering on the Chicago convention offer in retrospect a full-length study of extremism. Here, within the space of ten days we could watch the reactions of persons and groups against threat. This is the essence of extremism. Moreover, the mass media both reflected and contributed to expressions of extremist behavior.

David Ginsburg, director of the National Advisory Commission on Civil Disorders, criticized Mayor Daley, the Chicago police, demonstrators, and the news media for their roles in the rioting and other disorderly activities associated with those days and events. In each instance Ginsburg pointed to specifics which support the hypothesis that extremism is action, and particularly reaction and overreaction, under threat.[7]

---

[7] Daniel Walker, *Rights in Conflict: the Violent Confrontation of Demonstrators and Police in the Parks and Streets of Chicago during the Week of the Democratic National Convention of 1968: A Report Submitted by Daniel Walker, Director of the Chicago Study Team, to the National Commission on the Causes and Prevention of Violence* (New York: Bantam Books, 1968), p. 61. See also *New York Times*, August 22, 1968, p. 23; Sept. 10, 1968, p. 33.

With respect to the mass media, Ginsburg said:

> A balanced picture was not presented to the country. This was true of television, and it was true of the press as of the time. This is not to condone the police overreaction, but it is to say that the country was not told what the police faced.[8]

The Walker Report relates at least three instances in which claims were made that newsmen contributed to staged violence by photographing "encounters" between police and demonstrators.[9]

Three matters merit fuller and closer investigation as extremism in Chicago in August, 1968, is further analyzed.

One is the meeting of the Democratic National Convention itself, convening and proceeding under circumstances which bore frightening testimony to the sense of threat evident on every hand. Its setting was similar to an armed camp. The amphitheatre was surrounded by a protective fence. An elaborate security system was set up. Policemen, National Guard troops, plainclothesmen, and other security personnel privately employed by the convention were present in great strength. The *New York Times* declared, a week before the Convention began, "The Convention thus became, before it even convened, the first national political convention in memory to require the protection of troops."[10] At least two national television newsmen were attacked while on duty in the Convention hall.

A second matter which requires additional attention is the presence of diverse but generally leftist protest groups in the city of Chicago at the time of the convention. There were the Yippies, many of them high on drugs, practicing what one commentator called the politics of ecstasy.[11] Students for a Democratic Society, committed to the politics of confrontation, were there.

[8] David Ginsburg, *New York Times*, Sept. 10, 1968, p. 33.
[9] Walker, *op. cit.*, p. 303.
[10] *New York Times*, August 21, 1968, p. 32.
[11] Tom Buckley, "The Battle of Chicago: From the Yippies' Side," *New York Times Magazine*, September 15, 1968, p. 28.

Loosely knit coalitions were formed. "Among the dissidents ... were violent revolutionaries, pro-Peking sympathizers, communists, anarchists, militant extremists, ... pacifists, poor people's campaigners, civil rights workers and moderate left-wingers."[12] Among these, certainly, were extremists.

The confrontation between police and mass media personnel is a third matter which merits attention. Of about three hundred newsmen assigned to cover the parks and streets during convention week, more than sixty-five were involved in incidents with the police. Media personnel felt that the Chicago police were making it difficult for them to do their work. Following the convention the top executives of the ten largest newspapers, news magazines, and television networks sent Mayor Daley a sharply worded protest of the treatment of newsmen.[13] The Chicago Newspaper Guild declared that it would be "unsophisticated" to believe that none of the policemen involved "conspired with each other to wage planned mayhem on men serving as the public's eyes and ears."[14]

Thus, tragically, extremists and conditions favoring extreme reaction converged on an unfortunate city and the mass media took the brunt of it all.

Examples of Right-Wing Use of the Media

All the media of mass communication in America are vulnerable to extremist exploitation, for reasons already indicated. The evidence supports the conclusion that those forces to the right of the center utilize the mass media to a greater extent than do those to the left. This does not necessarily mean that the forces on the right have more sinister designs than do those on the left. It may mean that those on the right are better organized, better financed, and more aggressive in their use of the media.

Each week ten thousand right-wing radio broadcasts

[12] Walker, *op. cit.*, p. 17.
[13] *New York Times*, September 1, 1968, p. 34.
[14] *New York Times*, August 28, 1968, p. 36.

reach a listening audience of over twenty million people in this country. What are some of these? Who are their spokesmen and financial supporters?

Carl McIntire's "Twentieth Century Reformation Hour" is broadcast for a half hour each day, five days a week, on more than six hundred radio stations. McIntire, an ordained minister, was ousted by the Presbyterian Church in the USA in 1936 on charges of defamation of character, breaking "certain of the Ten Commandments," creating dissension, and stirring up suspicion and ill will. Following his expulsion he began his own organization. The position he voices on his broadcasts is racist, anti-Catholic, and strongly opposed to the National Council of Churches. Financing comes from a variety of sources, which ironically have shown no hesitancy to claim tax exemptions for contributions to a religious cause, despite McIntire's call for the repeal of the income tax.[15]

"Life Line" is associated with H. L. Hunt, a Texas billionaire who founded the Life Line Foundation in 1958, with Dan Smoot, who offers himself as an expert on communism and subversion, and with Dallas Bedford Lewis, who began sponsoring Smoot at a point when Smoot and Hunt appeared to be at odds with one another. Hunt's "Life Line" is heard on seven hundred radio stations for thirty minutes daily. "Dan Smoot Reports" has many additional radio and television outlets. These programs are financed by Hunt, Lewis, and, in a number of instances, by businessmen in the communities where the stations are located.[16] Rugged individualism and the evils of welfare, national government, and civil rights are recurring themes on these programs.

Billy James Hargis' "Christian Crusade" affords a good example of one organization's use of various media and also throws an interesting spotlight on methods of fund-raising. From his office in Tulsa, Billy James Hargis makes tape recordings and publishes two magazines, one of which claims a circulation of 130,000 and is seen by

[15] Arnold Forster and Benjamin R. Epstein, *Danger on the Right* (New York: Random House, 1964), pp. 100-102.
[16] *Ibid.*, pp. 135-140.

perhaps twice as many people. The thrust of the Christian Crusade's communication efforts is anticommunism. The number of stations broadcasting Hargis' programs has varied in recent years between a low of about fifty and a high of more than four hundred. At an annual convention of the Christian Crusade, Hargis raised, in an audience of seven hundred, a total of $38,870 to finance a six-month stint over the Mutual Broadcasting Company. Using a technique described by one reporter as a "prayer auction," Hargis prayed and begged until seventy-nine of those present had pledged the needed amount.[17]

Christian Economics is a biweekly tabloid newspaper published by the Christian Freedom Foundation and sent free to 200,000 Protestant ministers and laymen. This Foundation also produces a syndicated newspaper column which goes without charge to more than two hundred daily newpapers and twice as many weeklies. A radio program, "Howard Kerschner's Commentary on the News," is available to radio stations on a sustaining basis.

The themes of this Foundation's releases represent, in general, an elevation of laissez-faire, rugged individualism and private enterprise to the status of "Christian" economics. Social security has been described in this literature as "the older generation stealing from the younger." The income tax has been called "Communist doctrine." Labor unions have been described as "stemming from Socialism." Foreign aid and the United Nations have been interpreted as instruments for subsidizing and promoting Marxism.[18]

The Christian Freedom Foundation is supported almost entirely by J. Howard Pew of the Sun Oil Company and members of his family. In one five-year period, between 1958 and 1963, Pew and his family contributed more than a million dollars.[19]

No one knows the actual amount spent each year in

[17] *Ibid.*, pp. 69-86.
[18] *Ibid.*, pp. 267-268.
[19] *Ibid.*

promoting right-wing extremism. One authoritative source conservatively estimates $14,000,000 per year.[20] Where does this money come from? Seventy or more foundations (many of them tax-exempt), 113 business firms and corporations, 25 public utilities, and some 250 individuals were known to have contributed at least $500 each, according to one survey.[21] In addition there were many smaller contributions made by people of limited means as a result of direct appeals to "help save America" or "stamp out Communism."

Dealing with Extremism in the Mass Media

What are some positive ways to deal with extremism, left and right, as it manifests itself repeatedly in the mass media of communication?

In the first place, we need to be alert to the techniques of propaganda. Frequently employed propaganda techniques include the following.

The "plain folks" technique of identifying with the common man, the hard worker, the solid citizen, or the average guy, is an old, pervasive, and persuasive propagandistic device. Politicians have used it very successfully. Extremists also employ this method.

The use of the glittering generality is another effective propaganda device. The claim that college campuses are hotbeds of left-wing dissent is a glittering generality. Learn to ask, "Which college campuses? How many? Will you give specific details?" The glittering generality will be exposed for what it is in the seeking of specific information.

Name-calling or scapegoating is another device employed by extremists. To call someone a communist, a comsymp, or a fellow-traveller is to use this technique.

Stereotyping, or lumping, is a form of propaganda which categorizes as similar or synonymous groups or causes which may actually be quite dissimilar. The very term "extremist" is a stereotype. Qualifying terms such as "far left" and "far right" need to be added.

[20] *Ibid.*, p. 272.
[21] *Ibid.*, p. 279.

The simplistic solution to a complex problem is another propaganda device. The proposal of massive bombing of North Vietnam and the very different proposal of immediate, total withdrawal of United States forces are two examples of simplistic, essentially propagandistic devices.

A second series of suggestions for dealing with extremism in the mass media also centers on how to detect extremism. Learn to analyze an article, a news story, or a television or radio report. Is there evidence of slanting? Do value judgments appear in something that purports to be factual and objective? Does this item answer the basic questions of good communication; that is, does it tell, "Who? Where? What? When? Why?"

A third series of suggestions calls for more direct action. If there are evidences of extremism's use of the mass media, individuals and groups can and ought to counteract its influence.

Radio and television are regulated under law by the Federal Communications Commission. Licenses are granted for definite periods of time, and applications for renewal are subject to review. Complaints are investigated. If bias, distortion, or other practices are detected and the charges can be documented, a station can lose its license. This is a serious course of action and it should not be undertaken through malice or any other ulterior motive. But such drastic action may occasionally be called for. The provisions of the law and the procedures of the regulatory agency are provided for just this reason.

Radio and television personnel are also self-regulating through codes of ethics and professional organizations which they have created. These professional personnel and their organizations are very responsive to reactions from their public. When extremism appears in these media, attempts should be made to get the stations and personnel involved to correct the situations.

Inasmuch as radio and television are private enterprises operated for profit, these media personnel may, on occasion, allow extremist viewpoints to be expressed when time has been purchased. Concerned citizens may find it necessary to purchase time to counteract the extremist influence. In one such case a businessman purchased time for a one-minute recorded announcement in support of the United Nations to be broadcast immediately before and immediately after a program attacking the United Nations.

Individuals and groups should become familiar with and utilize the "fairness doctrine" applied by the Federal Communications Commission to the radio and television media. The essential point of this doctrine is this: if one viewpoint on a controversial issue of public importance is presented, the license-holder is required to make a reasonable effort to present the opposing viewpoint or viewpoints. This is to be done without regard to whether the issue is discussed in a paid or a free-time program.

Each radio or television station is required by law to make some free time available as a public service. Religious, educational, and cultural programs are often provided in the public interest without cost. Concerned individuals and groups should work with the media personnel in providing good programs.

One final suggestion, in dealing with all the media, is to accentuate the positive. When you read something you like, or find something on radio or television which meets with your approval, call or write the media personnel and express your appreciation and approval. Editors, program directors, commentators, and other media personnel report that people are quick to find fault but very slow to give praise.

Persons of goodwill, who represent reason and moderation, and especially Christians—who not only act on the basis of goodwill, reason, and restraint but follow the path of Christian love—should be on the frontiers of the communications field, both professionally and as recipients of mass communication. Herein lies the hope of doing something redemptive about the problems of extremism in the mass media.

8

The Gospel and Extremism

Thomas A. Bland

The gospel comes as good news to this frightened and fragmented world.

The gospel comes as the great good news of God's mighty act in Jesus Christ. This good news is committed to Christians, and we have unfinished business on our agenda: to declare the great good news in word and in act to an age which has been bombarded with disturbing, bad news. The gospel is good news of wholeness, especially suited for broken lives. The gospel is good news of freedom and sound-mindedness and release from fear to those who sit in darkness. It is good news of reconciliation for the alienated, the estranged, the lost.

The gospel, then, is God's good news to every person, including the extremist. Especially is the gospel good news to the extremist. He can, if he will hear and heed, free himself of the fear that causes him to overreact. He can put his trust in one who will not fail nor be discouraged until he has established justice in the earth (Isaiah 42:4). He can relax in the knowledge that vengeance belongs to the Lord and that man need not take this work of God into his own hands.

Thomas A. Bland is Professor of Christian Ethics and Sociology, Southeastern Baptist Theological Seminary, Wake Forest, North Carolina.

Moreover, any person, extremist or not, who responds to this good news will find his energies redirected and his life filled with new power which will enable him to give himself to the work of God in the world. No longer need he have his strength sapped, his attention divided, and his life committed to passing, unimportant matters. He can find peace that brings poise and strength that gives power for involvement in the revolutionary work of God in this world.

The good news of God for the extremist, therefore, is this: acceptance and commitment bring liberation from demons such as fear, hatred, and suspicion which haunt the extremist. In their place is the glorious liberty of the children of God (Romans 8:21). Moreover, the good news for all who will hear, obey, and respond is this: get busy in the revolutionary redemptive work of God in the world, an unfinished work which is nothing less than a new humanity created in Jesus Christ (Ephesians 2:14-16).

Good News About God

God is involved in a cosmic revolution whose end is redemption. The Sovereign Lord is at work in creation, in judgment, and in redemption, now and in all time.

The first word of good news to be addressed to our world is, therefore, good news about God. God, not man, is at the center of this world and of the good news. The Creator-God is the Sovereign Lord. This world, as it is, sin and all, evil and all, is still his world. He has not died and left us fatherless. He has not retired and left us without sustenance. He has not started something and left it to run down by some immutable laws while he sits back as an unmoved mover. He is sustaining what he creates.

It is precisely because of the good news of the Creator that we should regard our ministry in this world, now, to have very great importance. Sixty years ago, Walter Rauschenbusch wrote: "Ascetic Christianity called the world evil and left it. Humanity is waiting for a revolutionary Christianity which will call the world evil and change it."[1]

Some extremists, particularly of leftist persuasions, seem to have decided that Christianity in our day has called the world evil and left it, or at least left its massive human problems unattended. A mood of futility has settled upon some leftist extremists. Is their disillusionment with organized Christianity to be explained, if not justified, by Christians' failure to love, care for, and minister to this world in the name of the Creator?

Some rightist extremists, on the other hand, have embraced a faith quite contrary to the biblical affirmations of God's creating and sustaining activity. In holding to theories of the rulership of the world by evil conspiracies, rightists implicitly deny the sovereignty of God. In attempting to separate God from the world, some right-wing extremists have rejected the idea of God's purposive, continuing work in creation, governance, and redemption. Moreover, in place of the order and progression seen in biblical views of creation and of eschatology, right-wing extremists emphasize anarchy. The similarities of these teachings with gnostic heresies confronted by Christianity in its earliest centuries are striking.[2]

The good news about the Creator is that what he has created, he sustains. Christians should care about this world because it is God's world. To the dismay of extremists, both left and right, this entails that Christians should be at work in the world. God calls you and me to get busy with those very human problems of poverty, war, dehumanization, and racism.

The gospel is also good news about the Sovereign Lord who is active in judgment. Judgment is unavoidable. An affluent, spoiled generation does not want to hear about judgment. But it is inescapable.

[1] Walter Rauschenbusch, *Christianity and the Social Crisis*, ed. R. D. Cross (New York: Harper Torchbooks, 1964), p. 91.

[2] See the perceptive article, "The Faith of the Radical Right and Biblical Faith," by Glen Stassen, in *Review and Expositor*, vol. LXV, no. 3 (Summer, 1968), pp. 315-334.

THE GOSPEL AND EXTREMISM

We have traditionally emphasized judgment as an appointed day at the end of history. Biblical faith affirms that God has appointed a day on which he will judge the living and the dead and that every one of us must give an account of himself to God.

But there is more to judgment. Judgment is a process going on in history. Judgment is *now*! Today is judgment day! What we do now is related to the final judgment at the end of history. Matthew 25 suggests that there are going to be some surprises on that day, based on what we have or have not done on this day.

All of life stands under the judgment of God. It is all exposed to his righteousness. And it is all found wanting. Judgment begins at the house of God. The axe is laid at the root of the tree of religious traditions that have lost their vitality.

Every structure stands under judgment. The good news is that the Sovereign Lord will not tolerate idolatry. Here is where extremism comes under judgment. Any structure—nation, denomination, race, class, family, or anything else that demands or receives the ultimate loyalty of any person—is an idolatrous structure, and it stands doomed under the judgment of God. Ours is the task to declare this word of judgment.

Good News About Man

If the last word of the gospel were the word of judgment, we would be of all men most miserable. But the God who creates and judges also redeems.

God redeems! Here is the heart of the good news: "The beginning of the gospel of Jesus Christ, the Son of God: . . . Jesus came into Galilee, preaching the gospel of God, and saying, 'The time is fulfilled, and the kingdom of God is at hand; repent, and believe in the gospel' " (Mark 1:1, 14-15).

The good news of God in Jesus Christ the Redeemer is the point where God and man meet. For the gospel is good news about *man*.

The good news about man the *creature*, who bears the image of God but in his unregenerate state resents his creatureliness and seeks to become like God, is followed by the bad news that man is a *sinner*.

Every man is a sinner. Every dimension of man's life is touched by sin. The Bible depicts the religious dimension of sin as rebellion against God. The moral dimension of sin is man's inhumanity to man.

Extremists have an unrealistic doctrine of man. Those on the left often do not take sin seriously enough—their own or that of others. Those on the right often disregard the possibility of redemption. Both left and right dehumanize man, using persons as things. This is another manifestation of sin.

Man the sinner is confronted by Christ the Redeemer. Here the good news really becomes *good news*. God takes the initiative, in Christ, to reconcile the world to himself.

The gospel of redemption is revolutionary good news. God in Christ is bringing a new creation into fulfilment. "If any one is in Christ, he is a new creation; the old has passed away; behold, the new has come" (II Corinthians 5:17). A radical transformation takes place. A man in Christ has a new name, a new nature, a new reason for living, and a new sense of destiny.

The word addressed by our Lord to Nicodemus was a revolutionary word: "You must be born again" (John 3:7).

This radical redemption comes to man as both a gift and a demand. We have accepted the gift more often than the demand of the gospel.

Man is called upon to *repent*. To repent is to change one's perspective, one's outlook, one's actions. Have you noticed that Jesus called on religious people to repent? Repentance is a radical action. The gospel calls on man to live in a mood of repentance. This means, among other things, to keep one's mind open to God. A closed-minded man is an extremist. Moreover, he does not know how to repent.

Man is called upon to trust in the goodness of God and in the saving power of Jesus Christ. Jesus was most critical of the twelve because of their lack of trust. We need to pray today, "Lord, increase our faith" (Luke 17:5).

The gospel of redemption also brings the gift and the demand of *obedience*. "If any one would come after me, let him deny himself and take up his cross daily and follow me" (Luke 9:23). The martyred German theologian Dietrich Bonhoeffer said, "When Christ calls a man, he bids him come and die."[3]

The Pattern for Christian Life

When the good news is heard, received, and accepted, and when man repents, trusts, and obeys, he stands in a new relationship with Christ and with the world around him. He is to become radically involved in the work of one whom he has called Lord.

Elton Trueblood aptly describes the Christian:

> A Christian is a person who confesses that, amidst the manifold and confusing voices heard in the world, there is one Voice which supremely wins his full assent, uniting all his powers, intellectual and emotional, into a single pattern of self-giving. That Voice is Jesus Christ.[4]

The pattern of the Christian life is seen supremely in Jesus Christ. In him we see regard for truth and reverence for the human personality. Extremists and many others fall short here. The Christian both incarnates and does the truth. He refuses to resort to distortions of the truth through the "big lie," slanting, quoting out of context, or attributing sinister meanings and motives to others' statements and actions. Extremists are guilty of these and other kinds of distortions.

Furthermore, the Christian places high value on the human personality. Each person is regarded as a subject, not an object. Each person is a soul for whom Christ has died. Consequently, every effort to dehumanize persons,

[3] Dietrich Bonhoeffer, *The Cost of Discipleship*, rev. ed. (New York: Macmillan, 1959), p. 79.

[4] Elton Trueblood, *The Company of the Committed* (New York: Harper, 1961), p. 23.

to use them as objects, or to treat them cynically or cruelly is firmly resisted by the Christian in the name and spirit of Christ. Here, too, there is conflict with methods employed by extremists.

In attempting to give expression to the Christian life, present-day disciples need to recapture the sense of righteous indignation which motivated the Lord Jesus Christ. What, according to New Testament accounts, were the things that made Jesus angry?

Jesus did not respond with anger to the personal indignities to which he was subjected. However, he reacted with considerable indignation to certain kinds of exploitation of other persons.

For one thing, Jesus was indignant when religion was used for economic gain. One clear example is that he cleansed the temple of those who commercialized the central acts of worship (see Mark 11:15-19). When present-day extremists use the Christian faith, the Bible, or Christian institutions to sanction or to support their particular economic theories, Christians should react with appropriate indignation.

Jesus was also moved to anger when the more privileged took advantage of the less privileged and prevented their coming to him. This is most clearly seen in Jesus' rebuke to the disciples who tried to keep the children from coming to him (see Mark 10:14). He also condemned the attitudes and actions of religionists, especially Pharisees, who bound heavy, legalistic burdens around other people's necks. Is there a word here for some present-day religious extremists who make themselves the norm and exclude all who do not agree with them? In this connection, extreme fundamentalists and extreme liberals are often very close together in their methods. Firm, specific rejection of these extremists tactics is required today.

Jesus was also moved with anger when ossified religious institutions were allowed to get in the way of meeting human need. The laws concerning the sabbath included numerous examples. In the synagogue Jesus once asked those who had gathered, "Is it lawful on the sabbath to do good or to do harm, to save life or to kill?" (Mark 3:4). They were silent. Jesus healed a man with a withered hand. Our Lord, we are told, "looked around at them with anger, grieved at their hardness of heart" (Mark 3:5). In our day, we must not allow rigid institutionalism to keep us from meeting basic human needs. Are we, like Jesus, justified in being indignant with those who hide behind institutionalism in their failure to minister to human needs?

Our generation needs a rebirth of righteous indignation among Christians. Apathy, an uncaring and unfeeling mode of behavior, too often characterizes us. Some of the extremists, particularly on the left, have taken note of this and have written us off. We should make it impossible for them to do so any longer.[5]

The Christian Task Today

This revolutionary faith and way of life which is the Christian gospel is the power of God to save every person, including the extremist. Moreover, it calls Christians into fellowship in the church and sends them forth to alter those conditions in society which breed and nurture extremism.

We who hold an evangelical Christian faith will deny the Lord and his great good news if we fail to identify with the needs of this world and to seek Christian answers to these needs. Jesus Christ stands as the supreme reminder of God's way of meeting human need. He came on a salvation mission from God. He did not draw back from full involvement in human misery or from confrontation of those structures that deprived man of his humanity before God. If we are his faithful disciples, we must do the same.

As those of "the Way," as Christians, we will gladly join with those who do the truth and seek justice. In the struggle for justice we have many allies. The struggle should go on in the courthouse, in the schoolhouse, and, when the church is at its best, in the Lord's house.

---

[5] For an illuminating discussion of the anger of Jesus, see C. A. Anderson Scott, *New Testament Ethics: An Introduction* (Cambridge: University Press, 1948), especially pp. 26-47.

In our time, the struggle has gone on in peaceful protests against injustices, especially injustices of racial segregation. The decade of the 1960's witnessed the dramatization of these injustices through peaceful sit-ins at lunch counters and in other public accommodations. In 1964 the Civil Rights Act struck down the last vestiges of legalized segregation in public accommodations.

Some would condemn as an example of extremism the action of a group of white and Negro college students who began quiet sit-ins at lunch counters in Greensboro, North Carolina, in February, 1960. However, these young people were using peaceful means to protest against laws which they believed to be unjust. Let us remember that civil disobedience has been acknowledged in Christian thought from New Testament times. Let us also remember that the rights to dissent, to freedom of assembly, and to petition the government for redress of injustices are affirmed in our democracy under our Constitution and Bill of Rights.

This peaceful movement, this quest for justice, is in this writer's opinion in harmony with the best of Christian and of American democratic principles. In another's words:

> These young people ... are standing up for the American dream. The future rides with them as they ride forth into the advancing years of the twentieth century of a revolutionary world which struggles for the equal dignity of all people .... This youth movement had its origins not in Moscow but in Montgomery, Greensboro, Atlanta, Nashville, Knoxville, Rock Hill, New Orleans, Jackson .... This Southern youth movement is a present nonviolent expression of the on-going historic idealism of the American Revolution .... Its sources are in Carpenters' Hall, Philadelphia, and its farther headwaters are in the Judaean Hills where the carpenter's Son preached glad tidings to the disinherited of the earth and lived, died, and triumphed over death for the equal freedom, dignity, and hope of all persons as children of one God and brothers of all people on this earth, the fateful and hopeful home of the family of man.[6]

[6] From the Foreword to Merrill Proudfoot, *Diary of a Sit-In* (Chapel Hill: University of North Carolina Press, 1962), p. ix.

THE GOSPEL AND EXTREMISM

As Christians, we should of course exercise great care in joining forces with other groups in the struggle for justice. It is unquestionably our Christian duty, on the other hand, clearly to reject attitudes, teachings, tactics, and methods of extremism.

Fear, hatred, suspicion, and other attitudes which find expression in extremist groups are alien to the gospel of Jesus Christ. These attitudes lead to further alienation. They find expression in violence and other abrasive forms of social conflict. With these the gospel of love, of peace among men of goodwill, and of reconciliation between God and man and man and his fellows can have no traffic. The righteous wrath of God is turned upon these, and we Christians must clearly declare it.

The notion widely held among extremists that the end justifies the means is a diabolical lie. In one of our southern states, at a rally of the Ku Klux Klan, the Klud (chaplain) is reported to have denied that the Klan stands for violence. In impassioned tones he declared: "We are opposed to violence, and we're not going to stand for violence if we have to kill every nigger in the state." Other rightist groups, and leftist groups, too, advocate utilizing unethical means to achieve their ends. This will not stand the light of Christian truth. Both means and ends must be judged in the light of truth, justice, and love.

Views of man held by extremists are also directly challenged by the Christian gospel. When rightists declare that the church's concern is only for man's soul, they are denying the biblical view of man as a whole being, created in the image of God, with physical, emotional, social, intellectual, and spiritual needs. All these needs are the concern of the gospel and of the church. On the other hand, when leftists would turn the church into a political pressure agency solely concerned with restructuring society, they neglect man's eternal destiny. Man's ultimate problem is one which requires the saving grace of Jesus Christ, and man's final destiny is beyond this world and time.

Extremists distort history, and the corrective of a Christian view of history is needed. Rightists tend to resist change. They look back to the "good old days" and sing the virtues of a by-gone era—for example, that of nineteenth-century laissez-faire capitalism. Leftists, especially some of the so-called "New Left," deny the continuities of history. They seek to cut themselves off from the past. In many instances, they have no hope for the future. Ill content with the present, they are miserable.

The Christian regards the beginning and the end of history as God's activity. Moreover, God is active in the present and is moving history toward an end or goal. That goal is redemption. Between creation, which begins with God, and the consummation of the ages, which ends with God, there is bright, purposive hope. This word needs to be heard above the fatalism of the right and the futility of the left. The Christian hope as present reality and future expectation corrects the extremists' false notions of history.

Furthermore, many extremists betray an impatience which is an expression of sin. Many extremists want to throw off their finitude, become God, and have utopia now. To these it must be said that the city of earth will always be the city of evil. Even though the city of God has come down to dwell in the city of earth, there is no utopia and there will be none. Man's final and ultimate fulfilment lies beyond the city of man.

This does not mean, however, that we can do nothing. We can and should apply our God-given energies toward making this world what God wants it to be. In this connection, the second beatitude of our Lord has special meaning: "Blessed are those who mourn, for they shall be comforted" (Matthew 5:4). It is in our striving, in our partial successes, in our earnest longing for the Kingdom of God, that we are comforted.

Agents of Reconciliation

Our task as Christians, then, is to be ministers of reconciliation. We affirm with Paul: "Therefore, if any one is in Christ, he is a new creation; the old has passed

THE GOSPEL AND EXTREMISM

away; behold, the new has come." The Apostle continued:

> All this is from God, who through Christ reconciled us to himself and gave us the ministry of reconciliation; that is, God was in Christ reconciling the world to himself, not counting their trespasses against them, and entrusting to us the message of reconciliation. So we are ambassadors for Christ, God making his appeal through us. We beseech you on behalf of Christ, be reconciled to God. For our sake he made him to be sin who knew no sin, so that in him we might become the righteousness of God (II Corinthians 5:17-21).

There is the heart of the gospel! The gospel confronts extremists with the aim and goal of reconciliation. Reconciliation is costly. Think of what it cost God: the cross, his Son, our Savior. To be agents of reconciliation will be costly for us. To overcome estrangement, to end alienation, to preach and practice the peace of Christ among people who are waging civil wars, divided against themselves: this is difficult and costly.

To be ministers of reconciliation calls for commitment. We do not go alone. As Albert Schweitzer put it:

> He comes to us as One unknown, without a name, as of old, by the lake-side, He came to those men who knew Him not. He speaks the same word: "Follow thou me," and sets us to the tasks which He has to fulfill for our time. He commands. And to those who obey Him, whether they be wise or simple, He will reveal Himself in the toils, the conflicts, the sufferings which they shall pass through in His fellowship, and, as an ineffable mystery, they shall learn in their own experience Who He is.[7]

---

[7] Albert Schweitzer, *The Quest of the Historical Jesus* (London: Adam and Charles Black, 1910), p. 401.

9

Christians Coping with Extremism

William M. Pinson, Jr.

What answers have Christians for the problem of extremism? In a sense we have *the* answer—in Christ. Clearly the basic answer to extremism is the gospel, the good news. True, psychological and sociological as well as spiritual factors contribute to extremism. But if extremists will take seriously and respond fully to the good news, they will no longer have the psychological needs which often result in extremist personalities. And if Christians will commit themselves to the revolution called for by the good news, they will eliminate most of the sociological factors which create extremism.

But since few extremists respond fully to the good news, and since few Christians commit themselves to the social revolution called for by the gospel, we will no doubt have extremists to deal with for a long while. How, then, shall we go about coping with extremism?

Clearly we must do something, for extremism is contrary to the insights of the Christian faith and damaging to human life. Although the following suggestions for the Christian's response to extremism are by no means comprehensive, they indicate some approaches which can and should be taken.

William M. Pinson, Jr., is Associate Professor of Christian Ethics, Southwestern Baptist Theological Seminary, Fort Worth, Texas.

General Guidelines

In dealing with extremism some basic guidelines must be set forth before specific tactics and programs are developed. The following guidelines should be applied both to individuals and to groups.

(1) *Be realistic.* Extremism—under many labels—has been around for a long time. Its causes are complex; it will not easily be rooted out of American life. The best a Christian can hope for is to reduce or contain the problem, not eliminate it. Those who expect too much success may soon become discouraged and give up the struggle. Those who realize what they are up against will more likely stick to the task of coping with extremism.

(2) Steel yourself for hard knocks. Extremists by their very nature are tough, often unprincipled, opponents. If you are not willing to suffer abuse, threat, intimidation, harassment, character assassination, financial loss, and perhaps even physical harm to you or your family, don't enter the ranks of the active anti-extremists.

(3) *Desire to minister to the extremist.* Basically the Christian should not merely want to silence him. Being an extremist should not cut a person off from our love and concern. Make certain that your spirit and motives are in harmony with the Christian faith. Hate, love of combat, and vindictiveness have no place in the Christian life. Yet some anti-extremists who claim to be Christians display these traits—perhaps because of the tendency for a person to become similar in tactics and spirit to those whom he fights. Essentially the believer is to be not anti-extremist but pro-Christ. And because he is pro-Christ he should be for those things Christ is for—honesty, decency, justice, love—and against those things Christ is against—hate, fear, lying, disruption of men's lives for selfish gain.

(4) *Shun extremist tactics in fighting extremism.* Extremism is chiefly a method of social change, not an ideology. Extremism defines not so much content as attitude and tactics. Therefore if a person uses extremist tactics—regardless of the worthiness of his cause—he

becomes an extremist and contributes to the harm caused by extremism.

(5) *Define extremism carefully.* Many people think of it as extraordinary enthusiasm for a cause, and they can't understand why anyone is against extremism. It seems like a virtue, especially if the cause is worthy. Others use the word to describe those who disagree with their position; for them it is a label used indiscriminately to defame the character of an antagonist. The responsible person differentiates between liberalism, conservatism, and extremism.

(6) *Distinguish between types of extremists.* A hard-core extremist has a closed mind and selective hearing. He is simply not open to any facts or ideas which contradict his opinions. Although hope should be cherished for him and love extended to him, the most we can do may be to prevent his harming others. Many in the extremist camp, on the other hand, are rigid-minded but not closed-minded, and they are still open to reason. Dialogue, goodwill, and general openness of communication may bring these persons to a responsible stance.

(7) *Realize that extremism in the body politic, like pain in the human body, indicates that something is wrong.* To attempt to kill the pain without dealing with the basic cause is dangerous. Outbursts of extremist activity indicate that some people hurt badly and that fear and frustration are widespread. To write off extremist action as the work of a pack of kooks is to oversimplify the problem. Extremist activity often indicates that needed social change is taking place too slowly, if at all. The democratic process has not succeeded in dealing adequately with issues such as racism, social injustice, and poverty. How then do we as Christians propose to deal with these issues? Business as usual obviously is not the answer. And extremism, we believe, is ineffective and unjustified. We must therefore commit ourselves to develop an acceptable option for social change.

(8) *Deal in a responsible, democratic, and Christian way with problems raised by extremists.* Many of the issues they raise are legitimate: communism, injustice,

growing federal power, civil rights, sex education, war, and the quality of education. We are acting irresponsibly if we fail to deal with these issues for fear of being labeled extremists. And we can be sure that if legitimate tactics don't get results, illegitimate tactics will be used.

(9) *Discuss both aspects of extremism—left and right.* This will undermine charges that you are playing favorites or represent an extremist position yourself. If you attack only the right, you will probably be accused of being a left-winger or a communist.

(10) *Direct your effort primarily toward non-extremists.* The hope of altering an extremist is small: a total conversion of life is required, since extremism is a way of life. Anti-extremist material, however persuasive, will have little effect on a hard-core extremist. But it will diminish the extremist's influence on the ambivalent fringe and the concerned minority. The target group for anti-extremist materials, in other words, is the same as that for extremist materials.

(11) *Tailor anti-extremist materials to those whom you are addressing.* Liberals are more susceptible to left-wing extremist materials than are conservatives, while conservatives are more susceptible to right-wing propaganda. The material you present to a particular group should focus on the dangers and tactics of the brand of extremism to which that group is most susceptible. For example, material prepared for conservatives should discuss both right-wing and left-wing extremism to avoid any charge of bias. But authorities cited against right-wing extremism should be persons highly respected by conservatives.

(12) *Work both to curtail current extremist activity and to prevent future activity.* Existing extremist organizations must be contained, while the factors that produce extremist personalities must be eliminated. The sociological and psychological causes of extremism offer clues of how to avoid the development of extremists. Better homes and an improved social order will help. But it is also necessary to counteract the influence of organizations. Extremists in isolation can do little harm; organized, they can disrupt the democratic process and

curtail freedom. Individuals with certain types of personality may be potential extremists, but apart from the propaganda and recruiting activity of extremist organizations they may never become extremists.

(13) *Counter extremist propaganda.* This can be accomplished in several ways: expose extremists' tactics and thereby cut into the financial support for extremist propaganda; call for denial of tax-exempt status for extremist groups involved in partisan political action; ask for equal time on radio and television to counter extremist charges.

(14) *Expose the inadequacy of the extremists' oversimplified solutions to modern problems.* Public debate of significant issues by responsible persons is a necessary ingredient of democracy and a helpful antidote to extremism.

(15) *Encourage dialogue between liberals and conservatives.* These two broad political, economic, and religious groups should deal with their differences in open and responsible ways. This will make the center of American life more creative and may undermine extremist influence. Moreover, such open dialogue will demonstrate the complexity of real issues and expose the inadequacy of the extremists' simplistic solutions.

(16) *Involve all parts of society in dealing with extremism:* homes, schools, churches, labor unions, professional organizations, clubs, courts, mass media, special committees, fraternal groups—all can help. All are threatened by extremism and need to combat it.

(17) *Utilize both education and overt action.* Education is useful for molding attitudes and exposing the dangers of extremism. Most people, when they understand what extremism really is, will oppose it. Education can thus motivate action.

(18) *Become familiar with laws and government regulations useful in combating extremism*, such as libel and slander laws and the regulations of the Federal Communications Commission.

(19) *Train citizens to deal creatively with controversy.* People must be taught not to fear controversy, to

tackle obvious wrong, to speak out using accurate facts and statistics.

(20) *Never try to silence those who disagree with you.* Stress that what you oppose are underhanded, undemocratic techniques of handling disagreement. Emphasize that your primary objective is not to eliminate extremists but rather to promote the democratic process. Present a positive rather than a negative image. Make clear that you favor responsible controversy and welcome discussion about your position.

(21) *Recognize that the cure for extremism is not indifference to social problems but responsible, aggressive efforts to deal with them.* Because a person is excited about and active in dealing with controversial issues is no indication that he is an extremist; he may simply be legitimately concerned.

(22) *Point out the dangers of extremism as vividly and dramatically as possible.* The Overstreets, authorities on extremism, warn that

> ... unless we Americans get down to the task of appraising what extremist methods, of the left and right, lead to in the way of human sorrow and an erosion of the moral sense, we stand to lose the best that the centuries have given us.[1]

By sowing distrust and fear, extremists tend to paralyze positive, constructive efforts to build a better society. By their constant presentation of simple solutions to difficult problems, extremists undermine confidence in the government leaders who must grapple with all the complexities of the issues. By playing on prejudice and stirring up hate, extremists tend to divide Americans into warring camps. By intimidation, they drive all but the most stout-hearted to silence; thus issues which call for discussion receive no deliberation and truth remains undiscovered or unproclaimed. By clever propaganda, they dupe innocent persons into mouthing their slogans and joining extremist organizations. Their successes encourage others—both friend and foe—to employ extrem-

[1] Harry and Bonaro Overstreet, *The Strange Tactics of Extremism* (New York: W. W. Norton, 1964), p. 282.

ist tactics. Finally, their dogmatism discourages the study of real issues, such as communism, because extremists believe they know all they need to know about communism.[2]

(23) *Remember that the greatest allies of extremism are apathy and wishful thinking*, coupled with gullibility and selfishness, on the part of the majority. A minority can triumph over an apathetic majority.

Tactics and Programs

Extremism takes many forms. No one program to combat it will work in all situations. It seems to be easier to devise workable programs for dealing with the right than to do the same for the left, especially the New Left. Part of the reason is that the right is highly organized and operates in a fairly predictable pattern. The New Left, on the other hand, lacks concrete organization, constantly changes tactics, has no long-established leaders, and differs in emphasis from group to group. Also, anti-extremists have had more experience in dealing with the right than with the New Left.

Individuals and groups must exercise their own ingenuity in combating the problem. But the following suggestions will apply in a wide variety of cases and may spark creative thought in others.

The individual Christian can help cope with extremism in various ways. Here are some possibilities:

(1) Carefully study the tactics and programs of extremists. This will enable you to recognize and help counter extremist activity. (See the list at the end of the chapter for sources of information.)

(2) Challenge extremist tactics and statements whenever you encounter them. Don't fall for extremist propaganda; instead ask questions, call for clarification, insist on documented facts from responsible sources, and offer alternate interpretations for the facts. Learn to analyze extremist statements and materials.

[2] *Issues and Answers: Extremism.* Southern Baptist Christian Life Commission.

(3) Keep informed on current events from reliable sources. When wild charges are encountered, check the facts with responsible persons or organizations. Read from both liberal and conservative newspapers and magazines. Subscribe to the *New York Times* in order to have access to complete texts of speeches. In researching an issue, don't depend on popular magazines but investigate scholarly journals published by professional associations. Utilize books published by well-known companies more than those published by individuals or by organizations with a particular axe to grind.

(4) Don't pass on rumors or unverified information, particularly when it comes from sources suspected of being extremist. What "they"—the world's most often cited authority—say is not adequate documentation for the responsible Christian citizen.

(5) Support groups and persons working in a constructive and responsible way to deal with the problems and issues of society, including the problem of extremism.

(6) Maintain a healthy home to help prevent the development of extremist personalities.

(7) As a responsible citizen, take an active part in the democratic process. Vote, campaign for candidates, participate in party politics, express your views to public officials and be willing to serve in an elective or appointive office.

Churches can play a vital role in dealing with extremism, both within local congregations and through denominational agencies.

Local congregations in their regular programs of worship, ministry, education, evangelism, and social action can do much to curb extremism. The gospel, faithfully proclaimed and practiced, is the best antidote to extremism. In addition, local congregations can take specific action to deal with extremism, including the following:

(1) Don't allow the church buildings to be used for meetings of extremist groups.

(2) Prevent extremists from gaining control of church boards or organizations.

(3) If the pastor preaches the extremist line, a responsible group from the church leaders should discuss with him the importance of keeping extremist tactics out of the pulpit.

(4) Sponsor programs to discuss the tactics and dangers of extremism.

(5) Distribute materials which set forth the tactics and dangers of extremism. (See the list at end of this chapter.)

(6) Cooperate with other churches or with community organizations in efforts to expose and deal with extremists.

(7) Work to increase family stability; sponsor family life conferences; distribute family life materials; place books on the family in the church library; provide family counseling. Extremist personalities can be the product of an unhealthy home life.

(8) Encourage responsible citizenship through preaching, special programs, and distribution of literature, such as that available from the Christian Life Commission of the Southern Baptist Convention.

In addition to the work of local congregations, *denominational agencies* can aid in the struggle against extremism. For example, they can undertake the following:

(1) Prepare and distribute factual, readable, practical materials on extremism.

(2) Publish articles on extremism in denominational publications.

(3) Engage in research on extremism and distribute the findings in articles, pamphlets, and books. If research uncovers significant new developments in extremist activity, special bulletins or newsletters should be released to churches warning of these developments.

(4) Sponsor conferences and programs which deal with extremism.

(5) Engage responsible persons to speak on extremism at regular denominational conferences and conventions.

(6) Publish scholarly but readable books on extremism.

(7) Educate students in colleges and seminaries on extremism and responsible political action.

(8) Write and distribute materials to promote citizenship. This should include a "how to" book on Christian political action.

(9) Arrange for legal aid for churches and pastors under attack by extremists. Legal advice and counsel are often needed by those involved with extremists.

(10) If necessary, create a relief fund and information center to aid pastors who are dismissed from churches because of their efforts to deal with extremism.

(11) Develop an adequate program to assist churches in developing stable families.

Community groups also have an important role in countering extremism. The following suggestions have been made to help community groups—PTA's, civic clubs, schools, public libraries, and others—handle extremist attacks.[3]

(1) Do not wait until an attack has been made on your group before you begin to let others in the community know your organization's nature and purpose. If the reputation of your group has been established, false charges are less likely to be believed.

(2) Carefully consider any criticism of your group to determine what truth, if any, it contains. Extremists can be right.

(3) Maintain good relations with the press. Always supply them with accurate information. Don't be caught in halftruths, distortion, or misrepresentation.

(4) If an attack is serious enough to warrant a response, take your case to the public. Open charges deserve open responses. If an attack has been made over radio or television, write the station, state the date and program on which the charge was made, and request free time for rebuttal according to the provisions of the Federal Communications Commission. Send a carbon copy of the letter to the FCC, Washington, D.C.

---

[3] Overstreet, *op. cit.*, pp. 291-293; National Congress of Parents and Teachers, *Extremist Groups*.

(5) If you realize that persons who are extremists have infiltrated your group, assign them work which will acquaint them with the complexities of the problems with which you deal. This may demonstrate to them the inadequacy of their extremist position.

(6) Publicly challenge irresponsible tactics. Demand that charges be backed by facts, that generalities be filled in with specific content, that quotes used out of context and distorted statistics be explained.

(7) Demand that all charges be put into writing and signed.

(8) Don't back down in the face of extremist attacks in order to avoid controversy. This only encourages the extremist's attacks.

(9) If free speakers are offered to your group, ask that a summary of the speech and the credentials of the speaker be submitted in writing. Don't be afraid to look a gift horse in the mouth!

(10) If your organization handles printed materials or audio-visual aids, develop a selection procedure which will exclude extremist materials except to use them as examples of extremist tactics. Also have a definite policy on permitting announcements and passing out materials.

(11) Appoint a committee to study extremism and bring a factual report to the group. Devote a meeting to studying extremism—tactics, literature, and front organizations.

(12) Adopt bylaws and rules for parliamentary procedure. Be especially firm about the time and method for closing meetings; a favorite extremist tactic is to prolong a meeting until most people leave and then vote through the extremist program.

(13) Make it a rule that no resolution or motion introducing new business can be voted on until the meeting after it has been introduced.

(14) If in a meeting of your group an extremist attempts to disrupt proceedings, it is probably best to allow him to have his say. If he is obviously a kook, be calm and considerate in your response. His own tone and actions will undermine his appeal, and the less said

against him the better. On the other hand, if the extremist is smoothly persuasive, he should be dealt with and not allowed to take command of the meeting.

A number of specific community groups can be helpful in countering and preventing extremism. Among them the following deserve special mention.

Schools, especially public schools and colleges, are often victims of extremist attacks and therefore have a special interest in dealing with extremism. The following anti-extremist actions are possibilities for schools:

(1) Educate for insight so that students understand their own fears, their tendency to avoid blame by transferring it to others, and their desire to resolve problems, even wrongly, in order to escape the frustration of living with an unsolved problem.

(2) Help students understand other cultures and races by presenting scientific facts about racial groups and by developing racially integrated school programs.

(3) Teach students about the tactics, shortcomings, and dangers of extremism.

(4) Train students in how to handle controversy and how to deal with extremist personalities.

(5) Stress the importance and benefits of the democratic process. Urge students to work to improve the social order by exercising the opportunities open to them.

(6) Provide opportunities for college students to be involved in decisions concerning the school's program.

School boards and boards of trustees have a responsibility to protect teachers and administrators from extremist attack. This of course implies that such boards themselves must remain free from extremist control. They should undertake at least the following precautions:

(1) Draft a written statement of policy placing responsibility for curriculum decisions and selection of teaching materials with teachers, educational administrative officials, and, where appropriate, student representatives.

(2) Carry out an information program to increase community understanding of these policies.

(3) Have a clearly defined procedure for dealing with complaints on curriculum, books, teachers, policies, and programs. It is usually wise to insist that all complaints be made in writing and signed and to refer complaints to a special committee for study.

(4) Deal with student demands honestly and quickly. While no workable plan has been devised to deal with student demonstrations, in most cases decisive, restrained action has curtailed violence. Situations differ so radically that no single program or approach will fit each case.

Labor unions also have a role to play. In the past the labor movement was often labeled extremist. Today it is a generally accepted part of American life, and unions work to curb extremism. Union members should be active in their union and make sure that its leadership remains in the hands of responsible persons. If evidence of extremist infiltration appears, the union should take steps to educate members about the extremist group involved. If extremist materials are distributed, the union should distribute materials pointing out the dangers and tactics of extremists.

The business community should do its share in curbing extremism and giving financial and personal support to anti-extremist causes. Businessmen can also distribute information about extremism to their employees.

The mass media can aid in the battle against extremism. Newspapers should avoid supporting extremists and should inform the public about extremist tactics. Radio stations should balance their programing and not overexpose the public to extremist propaganda. They should also grant time for rebuttal to persons or groups attacked by extremists. Responsible, honest reporting of extremist outbursts and demonstrations is also needed.

Government at all levels bears a heavy responsibility for dealing with extremists. The FBI investigates many extremist groups; congress and state legislatures pass laws to curtail extremist tactics dangerous to the social order; government agencies distribute materials on extremism. But the government has a responsibility for positive action as well. Creative and extensive programs are needed to deal with poverty, discrimination, and injustice—factors that contribute to extremism. Government must become as concerned about justice as about law and order. Police forces, in particular, must be better staffed, better paid, and better trained to be more effective. They must relate better to all aspects of the community—including students, blacks, and the poor—and not overreact to threatening situations. Such overreaction feeds the flames of left-wing and black extremism.

Clubs and professional and fraternal organizations should also help combat extremism. Most American communities have a number of such organizations, many of which have national affiliations. Programs and distribution of materials on extremism should be a part of the activities of such groups.

Persons experienced in dealing with extremists insist that a *local anti-extremist coordinating committee* is essential to cope with extremism. Such a committee usually comes into being when a few individuals—sometimes just one person—become concerned enough to act. Unfortunately, an extremist outburst is often the factor which motivates the forming of the committee.

Most communities contain a number of persons with anti-extremist sympathies; these can form the nucleus of the committee. In developing the committee be sure to secure representation from the major segments of the community. Certainly a cross section of the community should be included: liberals, moderates, and conservatives; labor and management; religious persons and secularists; all racial and ethnic groups; educators and professionals; women's groups and men's clubs. Such a broad representation will keep the committee balanced, give it stature, and undermine criticism.

Anti-extremist committees differ vastly in organization and approach. Some are formally organized with constitution, bylaws, dues, and membership requirements. Others are informal gatherings of concerned persons. Some meet regularly; others come together only when there is special need.

If little headway is made in forming a committee with

extensive community representation, a few concerned persons may have to band together to do what they can. Often a handful of dedicated individuals can do a great deal.

The working group need not, and perhaps should not, be large. Ten persons bound together by a common dedication to the democratic process can do a great deal to thwart extremist efforts.

The first task for a local committee is to discover what extremist activities are already underway in the community. Here are some questions for which the committee should seek answers:

> Are school boards being subjected to undue pressure to revise school curricula? Have individual teachers been singled out for attack?
>
> Are libraries under pressure to add or remove certain books?
>
> Are any known extremist organizations represented in the community? If so, what is their program? Who are the members? (Sometimes the only way to discover the goals and programs of such organizations is to join them; but infiltration raises ethical problems for many Christians.)
>
> Are the newspapers receiving an unusual number of extremist letters?
>
> Are extremist materials being circulated in quantity? If so, what are the sources?
>
> Are local radio and television stations carrying biased announcements or commentary on the news, extremist programs, or call-in programs in which an unusual number of callers express the extremist line?
>
> Are any local bookstores centers for extremist propaganda?
>
> Have individuals been subject to character assassination or harassment because of stands they have taken on controversial issues?
>
> Does there seem to be extensive dissension in local political groups, with efforts made to discredit existing leadership?
>
> Have respected organizations been pressured to engage certain speakers or to follow a particular line on controversial issues?

CHRISTIANS COPING WITH EXTREMISM 147

Have special crusades or campaigns been held in the community on controversial issues? If so, who sponsored them? If "experts" were brought in, what were their credentials?

Some of the more active anti-extremist committees have prepared extensive files as the result of investigations and surveys of the community. These files cover persons or groups found to be active in extremist causes. Of course, most citizens are not skilled investigators and do not have time to conduct careful, extensive investigations. But by dividing up the chores, a group of citizens can find out a great deal about their community.

After the chief trouble spots have been located, the second step is to tackle specific issues to counter extremist activity. The committee must beware of entering the fray ill-prepared. Most extremists are skilled debaters. The committee should secure help from national organizations (see the list of organizations at the end of this chapter) and conduct research of its own.

The third step is to get the information on extremist activity to the public. The hope of democracy is that an informed public will ultimately reject undemocratic factions and programs. If a specific issue is at stake, such as police brutality or sex education in the schools, the information should deal with these specific issues. On the other hand, if no immediate extremist threat exists, the information campaign might relate to extremism in general, alerting the public to extremist tactics and dangers. The following can be used to reach the public:

(1) Meetings. If the anti-extremist committee is basically a coordinating committee for various community organizations, the representative from each group on the committee should urge his group to plan a program on extremism. In addition, special meetings open to the public should be planned. Such meetings should utilize expert program personnel. The format of the meeting may include speakers, a panel, a symposium, discussion—whatever best fits the need and the available resources. A word of warning is in order concerning such a meeting: many extremists are trained in the techniques of packing, disrupting, and taking over meetings. The

chairman must be prepared to thwart such efforts, thoroughly grounded in parliamentary procedure and able to keep firm control. Here are some suggestions to keep the meeting running smoothly:

> During discussion require that each person who speaks identify himself clearly.
>
> Demand that all who speak stick to the subject.
>
> Insist that each person abide by a previously announced time limit on individual questions or comments.
>
> Call for opposing opinions whenever a single viewpoint seems to dominate the discussion. It may be wise to have all questions submitted in writing, so that the chairman can screen out repetitive questions and those obviously intended to provoke rather than clarify.

(2) *Publicity.* Mass media are effectively utilized by extremists; they can also be utilized by those endeavoring to cope with extremism. All special meetings and programs dealing with extremism should be well publicized. It is important to maintain good relations with newspapers and radio and television stations. The following suggestions will help get the word out about extremism:

> Supply editors with clearly written news releases both before and after special meetings. Send your information at least a week prior to the meeting in a typed, double-spaced release, with the most important details in the first paragraph and other information following.
>
> Angle releases to different sections of a newspaper—editorial page, the women's section, business section, educational news.
>
> Write letters to the editor on key issues. Make certain that these letters are factual and to the point.
>
> Prepare spot announcements for television and radio and urge the stations to run them as a public service. If this fails, buy time.
>
> Utilize the Federal Communications Commission rule known as the "Fairness Doctrine," which requires broad-

casters to provide on request an opportunity for rebuttal of partisan views. The heart of the Commission's ruling is this:

> If one viewpoint of a controversial issue of public importance is presented, then the licensee is obligated to make a reasonable effort to present the other opposing viewpoint or viewpoints .... It is immaterial whether a particular program or viewpoint is presented under the label of "Americanism", "Anti-Communism" or "States' Right" or whether it is a paid announcement, official speech, editorial, or religious broadcast.

(Requests for free time under the "Fairness Doctrine" should be made in writing to the station, sending a copy to the Federal Communications Commission, Washington, D.C.)

Be alert for opportunities to utilize the hours which the FCC requires stations to use for "public service." Most stations are looking for good programs to fill these times.

Urge people to write stations that use anti-extremist materials and commend them for their action.

Distribute pamphlets, booklets, handbills, and other materials on extremism. Excellent literature is available from a number of national organizations. (See the list at the end of the chapter.) If you prepare your own material, steer clear of satire and cuteness; such devices are often misunderstood.

Prepare displays on democratic themes. Posters and displays can often be used in libraries, schools, community centers, and churches. Transportation centers and stores may also be willing to display posters.

Run carefully prepared newspaper advertisements carrying the endorsement of leading citizens. Such advertisements can be reprinted and used as leaflets.

(3) *Speakers Bureau.* The anti-extremist coordinating committee should train skilled speakers to present the case against extremism and for the democratic process. They should be made available at no cost to local clubs, PTA's, civic organizations, and schools. A summary of each speech and a description of the credentials of the speaker should be made available to such

organizations. These speakers must be factual, responsible, fair, and interesting in their presentation.

(4) Libraries. The committee should carefully check the libraries in the community to determine whether they have authoritative materials on extremism. If they do not, the committee should urge that such material be purchased or provide the material. If librarians are under pressure to stock extremist books and to exclude anti-extremist publications, the committee should counter this pressure.

Getting information on extremism in general to the public is important but not adequate. It is also important to develop specific tactics to counter extremist activities. The following are possibilities:

(1) Clearinghouse of facts. Needed in most communities is a clearinghouse for information on extremism. Armed with facts on publications, radio programs, organizations, and speakers, such a clearinghouse could supply valuable information to schools, clubs, and organizations who want to avoid unwitting use of extremist materials. It is impractical to have such a clearinghouse in every community, but regional offices would be very helpful. Universities or research centers are the logical locations for clearinghouses on extremism, but special offices may be required in some areas.

(2) Project Alert. After extremist organizations are located, it is important to keep tabs on them. This can be done by infiltration, or more simply by reading the newsletters and other publications of the central or national extremist organizations. When some new thrust or attack is indicated, the groups which will be affected should be alerted.

(3) Radio monitoring. Because of the extensive use of radio by extremists, particularly the right wing, radio stations carrying extremist broadcasts should be monitored. Whenever a personal attack is made on an organization or individual, those attacked should be notified and urged to request time for rebuttal under the FCC's "Fairness Doctrine."

(4) Analysis of extremist materials. Many people do not have the training, resources, or ability to analyze

and discredit extremist materials. It is important, therefore, that such analyses be done by competent persons and shared via newsletters and other means with the general public.

Extensive activity by an anti-extremist coordinating committee will cost a great deal. Potential sources of funds include cooperating organizations, interested national groups, and concerned individuals. By utilizing volunteer labor—students, teachers, housewives, and others—costs can be cut considerably.

Many of the programs and activities suggested for a local committee could also be carried on by a nationwide organization. A number of national organizations carry on some anti-extremist programs, but the Institute for American Democracy is apparently the only organization devoted primarily to combating extremism. Its program needs to be strengthened.

As indicated in the previous chapter, Christians have unique insights and resources for coping with extremism. We have, therefore, a special obligation to act. We know the nature of extremism and we have some idea of what we can do to deal with it.

Of course, we can retreat to the sanctuary of silence and refuse to speak or act. But such a course would be not just cowardly and irresponsible but a denial of our faith. Silence and inaction in the face of extremism is sin. As James put it, "So then, the man who does not do the good he knows he should do is guilty of sin" (James 4:17). We know much that needs to be done in the face of the extremist threat. Let us therefore act.

Sources of Information on Extremism

AFL-CIO, 815 Sixteenth Street, N.W., Washington, D.C. 20006.

American Association of University Professors, 1785 Massachusetts Avenue, N.W., Washington, D.C. 20036.

American Jewish Committee, 165 East Fifty-sixth Street, New York, New York 10022.

American Library Association, 50 East Huron Street, Chicago, Illinois 60611.

Anti-Defamation League, 315 Lexington Avenue, New York, New York 10016.

Center for the Study of Democratic Institutions, Box 4068, Santa Barbara, California 93103.

Christian Life Commission, Southern Baptist Convention, 460 James Robertson Parkway, Nashville, Tennessee 37219.

Democratic National Committee, 1730 K Street, N.W., Washington, D.C. 20006.

Group Research, Inc., 1404 New York Avenue, N.W., Washington, D.C. 20005.

Institute for American Democracy, Suite 101, 1330 Massachusetts Avenue, N.W., Washington, D.C. 20005.

National Congress of Parents and Teachers, 700 North Rush Street, Chicago, Illinois 60611.

National Council of the Churches of Christ, 475 Riverside Drive, New York, New York 10027.

National Education Association, 1201 Sixteenth Street, N.W., Washington, D.C. 20036.

Republican National Committee, 310 First Street, S.E., Washington, D.C. 20003.

United Nations Association, 345 East Forty-sixth Street, New York, New York 10017.

Helpful Materials on Extremism

Committee Handbook. A guide to forming a local committee to deal with extremism. $2.00. Institute for American Democracy, Inc., Suite 101, 1330 Massachusetts Avenue, N.W., Washington, D.C. 20005.

Countering Extremism. A brief pamphlet outlining tactics, dangers, and ways of coping with extremism. $.35.

What Is Extremism? A short introduction to extremism. Both from the American Jewish Committee, 165 East Fifty-sixth Street, New York, New York 10022.

Extremist Groups. A brief pamphlet with practical suggestions on what to do about extremist groups. $.15. National Congress of Parents and Teachers, 700 North Rush Street, Chicago, Illinois 60611.

Issues and Answers: Extremism. A small pamphlet setting forth the issue of extremism and how to cope with it. Contains a helpful, brief bibliography. 5 cents per copy — minimum order, $1.00. Christian Life Commission, 460 James Robertson Parkway, Nashville, Tennessee 37219.